An Absolute Massacre

An Absolute Massacre

The New Orleans
Race Riot of
July 30, 1866

James G. Hollandsworth, Jr.

)|(LOUISIANA STATE UNIVERSITY PRESS
Baton Rouge

First printing
10   09   08   07   06   05   04   03   02   01
5   4   3   2   1

Designer: Amanda McDonald Scallan
Typeface: Adobe Caslon and Caslon Open Face
Typesetter: Coghill Composition
Printer and binder: Thomson-Shore, Inc.

Library of Congress Cataloging-in-Publication Data

Hollandsworth, James G.
    An absolute massacre : the New Orleans race riot of July 30, 1866 / James G. Hollandsworth, Jr.
    p.   cm.
    Includes bibliographical references and index.
    ISBN 0-8071-2588-1 (cloth : alk. paper)
        1. New Orleans (La.)—History—19th century.   2. New Orleans (La.)—Race relations.
    3. Riots—Louisiana—New Orleans—History—19th century.
    4. Afro-Americans—Louisiana—New Orleans—History—19th century.   5. Louisiana—Politics
    and government—1865–1950.   6. Reconstruction—Louisiana.   I. Title.
    F379.N557 H65   2001
    976.3'34064—dc21   00-059675

The author is grateful for permission to quote from the Henry Clay Warmoth Diary, #752, in The
Southern Historical Collection, Wilson Library, The University of North Carolina at Chapel Hill.

The paper in this book meets the guidelines for permanence and durability of the Committee on
Production Guidelines for Book Longevity of the Council on Library Resources. ⊗

For a friend, mentor, and remarkable person, John D. Alcorn

The more information I obtain of the affair of the 30th in this city the more revolting it becomes. It was no riot; it was an absolute massacre.

—*P. H. Sheridan to U. S. Grant, August 2, 1866*

Contents

Contents

Illustrations

Acknowledgments

For their assistance during the research for this book I acknowledge in particular Mike Musick and Mike Meier at the National Archives; Joan Caldwell and Kevin Fontenot at the Howard-Tilton Memorial Library in New Orleans; and Wayne Everard at the New Orleans Public Library. I also acknowledge the encouragement and advice of colleagues at the University of Southern Mississippi: Brad Bond, Orazio Ciccarelli, William Kuskin, and Jan May.

Abbreviations

DCCL	*Debates in the Convention for the Revision and Amendment of the Constitution of the State of Louisiana* (New Orleans: W.R. Fish, 1864).
GJR	*Grand Jury Report, and the Evidence Taken by Them in Reference to the Great Riot in New Orleans, Louisiana, July 30, 1866* (New Orleans: Daily Crescent Office, [1866]).
HSCR	*House Report No. 16: Report of the Select Committee on New Orleans Riots*, 39th Cong., 2d sess. (Washington, D.C.: U.S. Government Printing Office, 1867; rpr. Freeport, N.Y.: Books for Libraries Press, 1971).
LC	Library of Congress, Washington, D.C.
MCR	*Executive Documents No. 68: New Orleans Riots*, 39th Cong., 2d sess. (Washington, D.C.: U.S. Government Printing Office, 1866).
NA	National Archives, Washington, D.C.
NYHS	New-York Historical Society, New York, N.Y.
OR	*War of the Rebellion: A Compilation of the Official Records of the Union and Confederate Armies*, 70 vols in 127 and index. Washington, D.C.: U.S. Government Printing Office, 1880–1901.

Abbreviations

RG	Record Group
SHC	Southern Historical Collection, University of North Carolina, Chapel Hill, N.C.

An Absolute Massacre

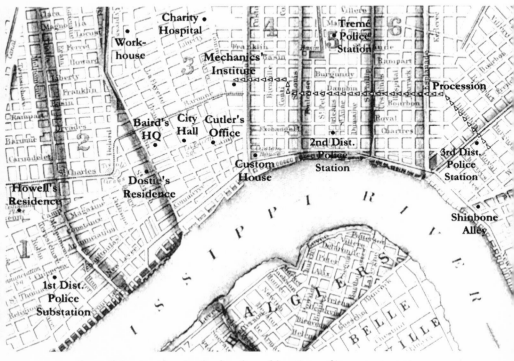

Area of the riot, showing landmarks and locations of important events.
Adapted from map of New Orleans (ca. 1860) by S. Augustus Mitchell

Introduction

T HE CIVIL WAR did not end at Appomattox. A second phase of the conflict began as thousands of erstwhile Confederates returned home and initiated a new struggle, the attempt to maintain the political and social dominance they had enjoyed during the war.

President Andrew Johnson's amnesty proclamation in May 1865 and the wholesale distribution of pardons in the months that followed enfranchised all but a handful of these rebels, allowing them to elect Confederate veterans and former secessionists to office. By the end of 1865, most southern states were under the control of the same men who had led these states out of the Union four years earlier.[1]

The return of former Confederates to power in Louisiana meant the ouster of Union loyalists who had been elected to political offices during the war. These were the men Abraham Lincoln had encouraged to set up a "Free State" government while secessionists were off fighting in the Confederate army or living as refugees beyond federal lines. But Lincoln's death had created a void that no one, least of all the new president, could fill. Lacking strong support

1. Eric Foner, *Reconstruction: America's Unfinished Revolution, 1863–1877* (New York: Harper & Row, 1988), 185–216.

or direction from Washington, Unionists in Louisiana were powerless to halt the erosion of the position they had gained during the war. Their weakness was highlighted in the fall of 1865, when a newly elected state legislature passed a series of laws to reinstate the oppressive Black Code that had been used before the war to control Louisiana's slave population.

During their brief tenure in office, Louisiana Unionists had not played the one card that might have kept them in power: black suffrage. Ever since emancipation, black males had hoped for, even expected, the right to vote. Although gaining the ballot would help them realize the promise of freedom and help ensure their civil rights, blacks had not been enfranchised. Even whites who had remained loyal to the Union during the war were reluctant to offer the ballot to citizens of African descent. But when former Confederates seized the reins of government, some Unionists realized that black suffrage was the one tactic they might use to stem the conservative tide.

The Unionist plan for enfranchising black males was notable for its simplicity. In April 1864, the military commander of the Department of the Gulf, Nathaniel P. Banks, had convened a convention to draft a new constitution for Louisiana. The document it produced abolished slavery but left the question of black suffrage to the legislature. The Free State legislature that assembled in 1865 under the provisions of the new constitution had failed to offer black males the vote, and the conservative legislature that convened in 1866 was unwilling to consider the issue. Nevertheless, members of the constitutional convention who favored black suffrage refused to give up. The motion to adjourn the convention of 1864 had provided that the body could reconvene at a later date. Seizing on this parliamentary oversight, a handful of former delegates decided to bypass the legislature by reconvening the convention and amending the constitution to disfranchise former Confederates and enfranchise blacks.

Most whites in Louisiana believed that reconvening the constitutional convention was illegal and that this blatant bid for power would surely fail in the courts. Although some people thought that it would be best to ignore these proceedings, many white Louisianians did not like the idea of promoting black suffrage, regardless of its chances for success. Conflict seemed inevitable when the convention reconvened at the Mechanics' Institute on Monday, July 30, 1866.[2]

The convention's president pro tem called the delegates to order at noon.

2. George C. Rable, *But There Was No Peace: The Role of Violence in the Politics of Reconstruction* (Athens: University of Georgia Press, 1984), 46–49.

Outside, a large crowd of hostile whites gathered in the streets around the building. A procession of black convention supporters on their way to the institute pushed through the angry throng. Words were exchanged between the marchers and members of the crowd, shots rang out, and within minutes a riot erupted with unrestrained fury. By the time the army intervened later that afternoon, at least forty-eight men were dead, and more than two hundred had been wounded.[3]

The New Orleans riot ignited a new conflict that raged for more than a decade and thus became to the second phase of the Civil War what Fort Sumter was to the first. But this time the rebels won, and the result of that victory was the establishment of a politically cohesive region, the "Solid South." Although the Confederacy had lasted only four years, the South that emerged from Reconstruction was to last almost a hundred.[4]

The causes of the New Orleans riot were as complex and interrelated as its consequences. Some of the reasons for its eruption were the postwar struggle for political control of the state government, the uncertain authority of the Union army of occupation, the deterioration of social restraint in a community demoralized and divided as a result of the war, the inconsistent and confusing intervention of federal authority from Washington, the persistent and aggressive efforts of many Louisianians to rehabilitate the doctrine of white supremacy, and the emergence of a vocal and well-organized protest movement made up primarily of black citizens whose expectations for civil rights clashed with the racism of local whites.

Despite the many factors contributing to this violent outburst, accounts of the riot over the past 130 years have tended to blame one side or the other.

---

3. There have been numerous race-related riots in the United States: Memphis (1866), Atlanta (1905), Springfield (1908), East St. Louis (1917), Houston (1917), Chicago (1919 and 1965), Omaha (1919), Harlem (1943), Detroit (1943 and 1967), Rochester (1964), San Francisco (1966), Boston (1967), Newark (1967), Washington, D.C. (1968), and Los Angeles (1965 and 1992) (Allen D. Grimshaw, *Racial Violence in the United States* [Chicago: Aldine, 1969], xv–xvii, 313). The worst of these was probably the New York draft riots in July 1863, when 119 people were killed and large portions of the city burned to the ground (Adrian Cook, *The Armies of the Streets: The New York City Draft Riots of 1863* [Lexington: University of Kentucky Press, 1974], 213–32).

4. Earl Black and Merle Black, *Politics and Society in the South* (Cambridge, Mass.: Harvard University Press, 1987); William Gillette, *Retreat from Reconstruction, 1869–1879* (Baton Rouge: Louisiana State University Press, 1979), 378–80; Dewey W. Grantham, *The Life and Death of the Solid South: A Political History* (Lexington: University Press of Kentucky, 1988), and Rable, *But There Was No Peace.*

Among these one-sided explanations are those by the pro-Confederate historian Charles G. Bowers, who blamed a "revolutionary band of Radicals," and W. E. B. Du Bois, who believed that the riot was the result of a "deliberate plan of the city fathers." Although a few accounts have implicated both sides, only one author, Joseph G. Dawson, has stated unequivocally that "all of those involved had to share the blame for the riot."[5]

This book chronicles the riot's complex causes. It is about people who allowed prejudice, intolerance, and self-interest to overrule common sense and fair play. From this perspective, there were no villains and no heroes, for everyone who participated in the deadly affair was both victim and instigator.

It takes a remarkable person to set aside animosities of the past and work constructively for a new order in which harmony and cooperation rule the day. The real tragedy of the riot in New Orleans on July 30, 1866, was that the remarkable people stayed home.

5. Charles G. Bowers, *The Tragic Era: The Revolution After Lincoln* (Boston: Houghton Mifflin, 1957), 127; W. E. B. Du Bois, *Black Reconstruction in America* (New York: Russell & Russell, 1962), 464–66; Howard K. Beale, *The Critical Year: A Study of Andrew Johnson and Reconstruction* (New York: Frederick Ungue, 1958), 353; Rable, *But There Was No Peace*, 46–58; Joseph G. Dawson, *Army Generals and Reconstruction: Louisiana, 1862–1877* (Baton Rouge: Louisiana State University Press, 1982), 40.

Give Us a Free State

MURDER? Octave Breaux strained to catch the conversation. Less than six feet separated Breaux from two men talking on the other side of the fence that surrounded his small garden.

It was four o'clock, Friday morning, July 27, 1866, and the first hint of dawn had yet to break the hot summer night. Breaux had gotten up early and made his way through the darkness of the house on the corner of Johnson and Lapeyrouse Streets to the garden in back where he kept a few goats. The fence around the garden provided some privacy, and the two men on the other side were unaware of his presence.[1]

One of the men was standing on the banquette; the other was seated in a carriage next to the curb. Breaux could catch only snatches of the conversation. "Why?" the man on the banquette asked. "Because the niggers want to amend the constitution, and we have to find a way to keep them from assembling," the man in the carriage responded. Breaux knew immediately that the two men were talking about the constitutional convention scheduled to reconvene

---

1. The location of Breaux's house comes from Durant's testimony in *HSCR*, 8. Durant indicated "the corner of Jackson and La Peyrouse," but Johnson Street, not Jackson, intersects Lapeyrouse.

in New Orleans on Monday. "If you want to join us," the man in the carriage continued, "we would like to have you." "I will," the other declared. The man in the carriage offered a sheet of paper for the other to sign. Breaux leaned forward to glimpse the document through a chink in the fence, but it was too dark. Suddenly, Breaux sneezed. Quickly the man on the banquette stepped into the carriage, and the two men drove away.[2]

Octave Breaux was a black creole who earned his living as a painter. He did not speak English very well, but he understood clearly what the two men had been talking about. Everyone knew about the convention, which had been called to discuss the prospect of an electoral franchise for all males, regardless of race. Blacks saw suffrage as their one chance to make good on the promise of emancipation. Whites were opposed to giving black men the vote and were determined to prevent the convention from amending the constitution to accomplish this goal.

Breaux understood the white opposition well. He had enlisted in the Louisiana Native Guards, the first regiment of black soldiers in the Union army, and had fought against the Confederates for three years. He had been with the Native Guards at Port Hudson when they had charged the rebels behind deep entrenchments on top of a steep bluff. The black soldiers had been pinned down behind stumps and fallen trees while Confederate marksmen made the ground a killing field. When darkness came, the black soldiers had been able finally to slip away. Although casualties in white Union regiments had been removed under a flag of truce after the battle, the black dead were left where they fell. The bodies had lain in front of the Confederate breastworks for weeks until the stench of their decay made even the rebels anxious to get them beneath the ground.[3]

Now, with this talk of further bloodshed, Breaux knew that he had to warn the authorities about the plot to prevent the convention from reconvening. At half past eight on Friday morning, Breaux went to see General Absalom Baird, head of the Freedmen's Bureau in New Orleans. Baird's adjutant came out to talk with the black man. "General Baird is not in," he told Breaux. Disappointed, Breaux set out for the headquarters of General Philip H. Sheridan, the military commander of Louisiana and Texas. A lieutenant came out to meet him. General Sheridan was not in, the officer said; he had left for Texas

2. *HSCR*, 232–33. A banquette is a sidewalk.

3. Compiled military service record for Corporal Octave Breaux, NA. For the assault of the 1st Native Guards at Port Hudson, see James G. Hollandsworth, *The Louisiana Native Guards: The Black Military Experience in the Civil War* (Baton Rouge: Louisiana State University Press, 1995).

four days earlier. Breaux told the lieutenant what he had overheard and then, having done his duty, returned home.[4]

The constitutional convention had been moribund for almost two years by the time Octave Breaux overheard the two men plotting outside his garden. Completing its work in July 1864, the convention had been an important step in a process by which Louisiana Unionists hoped the state could be readmitted to the Union.

That process had begun almost as soon as the federal army occupied New Orleans in May 1862. With the encouragement and support of the federal commander, Benjamin F. Butler, citizens with Unionist sentiments came forward, singly and in groups, to renew their allegiance to the "Old Flag." By June, enough people had affirmed their loyalty to warrant the formation of a Union Association, which became the basis for Unionist activity for more than a year.[5]

Abraham Lincoln was eager to capitalize on the reemergence of support for the Union in Louisiana. In November, he authorized the military governor, Brigadier General George F. Shepley, to hold elections for two representatives from congressional districts partially under Union control. Benjamin F. Flanders, a transplanted New Englander who had lived in New Orleans for almost twenty years, won the seat in the first congressional district. Michael Hahn, a thirty-two-year-old lawyer who had arrived in New Orleans as a child with his family from Germany, captured the second with 55 percent of the vote.[6]

Despite his initial success in mobilizing Unionist sentiment, Butler's iron-fisted rule of New Orleans created ill-will and dissatisfaction among the pro-

---

4. *HSCR*, 232–33.

5. Gilles Vandal, "The New Orleans Riot of 1866: The Anatomy of a Tragedy" (Ph.D. dissertation, College of William and Mary, 1978), 3; *New Orleans Daily Delta*, June 7, 1862; also see "The Record of Michael Hahn," *New Orleans Era*, January 31, 1864. Vandal's dissertation was published under the title *Anatomy of a Tragedy: The New Orleans Riot of 1866* (Lafayette, La.: Center for Louisiana Studies, 1986).

6. Lincoln to Shepley, November 21, 1862, in Roy P. Basler, ed., *The Collected Works of Abraham Lincoln*, 9 vols. (New Brunswick, N.J.: Rutgers University Press, 1953–55), 5:504–5; Herman Belz, *Reconstructing the Union: Theory and Policy During the Civil War* (Ithaca, N.Y.: Cornell University Press, 1969), 106–7; *New York Times*, December 12, 1862; Peyton McCrary, *Abraham Lincoln and Reconstruction: The Louisiana Experiment* (Princeton, N.J.: Princeton University Press, 1978), 58, 99–100, 107; Hans L. Trefousse, *Historical Dictionary of Reconstruction* (New York: Greenwood Press, 1991), 99–100. Hahn was born in Klinenmünster, Bavaria, in 1830 (Amos E. Simpson and Vaughn Baker, "Michael Hahn: Steady Patriot," *Louisiana History* 13 [Summer 1972]: 229).

Confederate population in the city. Lincoln knew that this contingent would not voluntarily reassert their loyalty to the Union unless he could convince them that accepting federal jurisdiction was preferable to secession. Hoping that a more conciliatory approach might help, Lincoln named Nathaniel P. Banks, a skillful politician from Massachusetts and major general in the Union army, to replace Butler.[7]

Banks arrived in New Orleans in mid-December 1862 and immediately set out to implement a new policy of cooperation and conciliation. "There had been harsh measures enough in this department," one of Banks's aides explained, "and since Butler had stroked the cat from the tail to head, and found her full of yawl and scratch, [Banks] was determined to stroke her from head to tail, and see if she would hide her claws, and commence to purr."[8]

It appeared at first that Banks's new policy might succeed. Planters liked Banks's labor plan, which put slaves back to work on the plantations, and local businessmen endorsed the steps Banks took to encourage commerce and to reopen trade with the North. "The merchants are doing more business every day," Banks wrote to his wife two months after his arrival. "The ladies and children are out in the street and all are feeling well. All the people seem to think well of me—even the thieves take off their hats."[9]

Pleased with his success, Banks encouraged Unionists to organize a permanent political party, one that would provide a foundation on which Louisiana could be readmitted to the Union. On May 8, 1863, delegates from the several Unionist clubs in the city and parishes under federal control assembled in New Orleans to form the Free State of Louisiana.[10]

The chairman of the Free State meeting was Thomas Jefferson Durant. "Tall, thin, sallow, [and] cadaverous," Durant was a Philadelphia native who had come to New Orleans in 1831 as a young man. A powerful orator and shrewd lawyer, Durant had made a name for himself in New Orleans. He had

7. LaWanda Cox, *Lincoln and Black Freedom: A Study in Presidential Leadership* (Columbia: University of South Carolina Press, 1981), 52; McCrary, *Lincoln and Reconstruction*, 108.

8. General Orders Nos. 113, 114, 117, 120, 121, December 20–28, 1862, *OR*, 15:615–26; George H. Hepworth, *The Whip, Hoe, and Sword; or, The Gulf-Department in '63* (Boston: Walker, Wise, 1864), 27–28. See also Fred Harvey Harrington, *Fighting Politician: Major General N. P. Banks* (Philadelphia: University of Pennsylvania Press, 1948), and James G. Hollandsworth, *Pretense of Glory: The Life of General Nathaniel P. Banks* (Baton Rouge: Louisiana State University Press, 1998).

9. Banks to Mary Banks, February 24, 1863, Nathaniel P. Banks Collection, LC.

10. *New Orleans Era*, April 26, May 13, 1863; McCrary, *Lincoln and Reconstruction*, 129–30; "Minutes of General Committee of Union Associations, May 19, 1863," NYHS.

kept a low profile while the secessionists were in charge but let his loyalist sentiments be known after federal troops arrived. With Flanders and Hahn away in Washington, Durant had become the unchallenged leader of the Unionist movement in New Orleans.[11]

The key to the Free State platform was a call for a constitutional convention to draft a document under which Louisiana could be readmitted to the Union. Military Governor Shepley liked the idea and named Durant state attorney general with authority to register "all free white male citizens" in preparation for an election of delegates as soon as General Banks gave the word.[12]

Lincoln also was pleased that supporters of the Free State were ready "to make a new constitution recognizing the emancipation proclamation and adopting emancipation in those parts of the state to which the proclamation does not apply." To expedite the process, Lincoln urged Banks on August 5, 1863, to "confer with intelligent and trusty citizens of the state, among whom I would suggest Messrs. Flanders, Hahn, and Durant." Speed was of great importance, for Lincoln wanted a new constitution for Louisiana by the time Congress convened in December 1863.[13]

Durant was eager to follow through on Lincoln's directive, but Banks was not. Banks's cooperation was crucial because Durant did not have funds to carry out the registration on his own and needed transportation and protection from the army, especially in the parishes outside of the city. As a result, the registration of voters for the constitutional convention proceeded slowly.[14]

There were two reasons why Banks failed to support Durant in his attempt

11. [Judge Whitaker], *Sketches of Life and Character in Louisiana* (New Orleans: Ferguson & Crosby, 1847), 23–24; C. Peter Ripley, *Slaves and Freedmen in Civil War Louisiana* (Baton Rouge: Louisiana State University Press, 1976), 161; Trefousse, *Historical Dictionary of Reconstruction*, 66; McCrary, *Lincoln and Reconstruction*, 99, 125; Durant to Butler, February 20, 1865, Benjamin F. Butler Papers, LC. A slaveholder himself, Durant did not free his slaves, a forty-six-year-old woman and her children, until March 1863, three months after the Emancipation Proclamation went into effect (Joseph G. Tregle, "Thomas J. Durant, Utopian Socialism, and the Failure of Presidential Reconstruction in Louisiana," *Journal of Southern History* 45 [November 1979]: 499).

12. Shepley, Gen. Order No. 24, *New Orleans Daily Picayune*, June 14, 1863; Belz, *Reconstructing the Union*, 144.

13. Lincoln to Banks, August 5, 1863, in Basler, ed., *Collected Works of Abraham Lincoln*, 6:364–66; Belz, *Reconstructing the Union*, 146.

14. Tregle, "Thomas J. Durant," 505; McCrary, *Lincoln and Reconstruction*, 161–62; Philip D. Uzee, "The Beginnings of the Louisiana Republican Party," *Louisiana History* 12 (Summer 1971): 201. Banks may have also been irritated by Durant's refusal to bring him into his confidence (Ted Tunnell, *Crucible of Reconstruction: War, Radicalism, and Race in Louisiana, 1862–1877* [Baton Rouge: Louisiana State University Press, 1984], 46).

to register loyal white males during the fall of 1863. For one, Banks was distracted with his grand design to wrest control of Texas from the Confederates by lodging a series of armed enclaves along the coast. But there was more to his hesitancy than the distractions of a military campaign. Nathaniel P. Banks had become disenchanted with Thomas Jefferson Durant.[15]

The reason for Banks's disenchantment was Durant's idea of what the Free State of Louisiana should be like after it was "reconstructed." Durant's view was much more radical than what Banks had in mind. Rather than favoring a state government composed of Unionists who shared the sentiments of the old planter elite, Durant was committed to a complete restructuring of the southern way of life. Such a reconstruction included not only the abolition of slavery but also the right of black men to vote.[16]

Initially, Durant's call for black suffrage had been limited to black men who had been free before the war. New Orleans contained the largest, the wealthiest, and the best-educated community of free blacks in the country. Not even New York City could boast of having more black "doctors, dentists. . . . silversmiths, portrait-painters, architects, brick-layers, plasterers, carpenters, tailors, cigar-makers, &c." "Hommes de couleur libre," as free blacks were called in New Orleans, enjoyed privileges not afforded blacks elsewhere in the South, allowing them by 1860 to accumulate more than $2 million worth of property.[17]

On the issue of black suffrage, the free black community had led the way.

15. McCrary, *Lincoln and Reconstruction*, 200–201; Tunnell, *Crucible of Reconstruction*, 43.

16. McCrary, *Lincoln and Reconstruction*, 184–85, 228–29; Tregle, "Thomas J. Durant," 488–91; Tunnell, *Crucible of Reconstruction*, 28, 37, 53. Durant was dedicated to the ideals of utopian socialism, particularly those expressed by the French physicist and mathematician François Marie Charles Fourier. Like Fourier, Durant believed that a flawed society, particularly as it existed in the southern United States, could not be fixed by run-of-the-mill reforms (see Joseph G. Tregle, "Thomas J. Durant," 490–95).

17. Roland C. McConnell, "Louisiana's Black Military History," in *Louisiana's Black Heritage*, ed. Robert R. MacDonald, John R. Kemp, and Edward F. Haas (New Orleans: Louisiana State Museum, 1979), 48; Tunnell, *Crucible of Reconstruction*, 19, 67–68; Manoj K. Joshi and Joseph P. Reidy, "To Come Forward and Aid in Putting Down This Unholy Rebellion": The Officers of Louisiana's Free Black Native Guard During the Civil War Era," *Southern Studies* 11 (1982): 327; Finian P. Leavens, "*L'Union* and the New Orleans *Tribune* and Louisiana Reconstruction" (M.A. thesis, Louisiana State University, 1966), 3; also see Arthé Agnes Anthony, "The Negro Creole Community in New Orleans, 1880–1920: An Oral History" (Ph.D. dissertation, University of California, Irvine, 1978), 28; Robert C. Reinders, *End of an Era: New Orleans, 1850–1860* (New Orleans: Pelican, 1964), 23. The comparison with New York City comes from Ulrich Bonnell Phillips, *American Negro Slavery: A Survey of the Supply, Employment and Control*

In late September 1862, Paul Trévigne, a prominent free man of color who had taught language in a Catholic school for black children before the war, began editing *L'Union*, a biweekly French-language newspaper that issued a clarion call for civil rights for free blacks. "We inaugurate today a new era in the South," Trévigne wrote in *L'Union*'s salutatory editorial. "We proclaim the Declaration of Independence as the basis of our platform. . . . You who aspire to establish true republicanism, democracy without shackles, gather around us and contribute your grain of sand to the construction of the Temple of Liberty!" *L'Union* continued to press for free black suffrage throughout 1862 and into 1863 and, as a result, had been instrumental in swaying a majority of free blacks in New Orleans to Trévigne's point of view.[18]

On November 5, 1863, an enthusiastic crowd of free blacks converged on the Economy Hall for a rally to promote suffrage for free men of color. Some of the speakers were white men, Unionists who sought to establish a common cause with their free black neighbors. But free black leaders set the tone. "They did not ask for social equality, and did not expect it," P. B. S. Pinchback, a former captain in the Louisiana Native Guards, told the audience, "but they [free blacks in New Orleans] demanded political rights—they wanted to become men."[19]

Durant went public with his endorsement for free black suffrage the next month. Banks was not surprised, for he had distrusted Durant's agenda all along, and Banks was afraid that a white backlash to Durant's radical ideas would scuttle his plan to coax Louisiana back into the Union. If such an out-

---

of Negro Labor as Determined by the Plantation Regime (1918; rpr. Baton Rouge: Louisiana State University Press, 1966), 438–39.

18. William P. Connor, "Reconstruction Rebels: The *New Orleans Tribune* in Post-War Louisiana," *Louisiana History* 21 (Spring 1980): 161; Jean-Charles Houzeau, *My Passage at the New Orleans* Tribune: *A Memoir of the Civil War Era*, ed. David G. Rankin, trans. Gerard F. Denault (Baton Rouge: Louisiana State University Press, 1984), 71; Joseph Logsdon and Caryn Cossé Bell, "The Americanization of Black New Orleans, 1850–1900," in *Creole New Orleans: Race and Americanization*, ed. Arnold R. Hirsch and Joseph Logsdon (Baton Rouge: Louisiana State University Press, 1992), 222–25; Caryn Cossé Bell, *Revolution, Romanticism, and the Afro-Creole Protest Tradition in Louisiana, 1718–1868* (Baton Rouge: Louisiana State University Press, 1997), 226–27; Tunnell, *Crucible of Reconstruction*, 75; *L'Union*, September 27, 1862, as translated in James McPherson, *The Negro's Civil War: How American Blacks Felt and Acted During the War for the Union* (1965; rpr. New York: Ballantine, 1991), 280.

19. "A Meeting of Free Colored Citizens at Economy Hall," *New Orleans Times*, November 6, 1863. For an extended discussion of the Afro-Creole influence on the free black community in New Orleans, particularly in regard to radical opinion, see Logsdon and Bell, "Americanization of Black New Orleans," and Bell, *Revolution, Romanticism, and the Afro-Creole Protest Tradition*.

come would be unfortunate for the state, it would be disastrous for Banks personally. Banks had his eyes set on the White House, and a failure in Louisiana would seriously undercut his prospects when the Republicans nominated their candidate for president in 1864.[20]

Exasperated by Banks's lack of cooperation, Durant had written directly to Lincoln on October 1, 1863. "You appear to think that a Registration of voters is going on under my supervision, with the view of bringing on the election of delegates to a Constitutional Convention," he wrote, "but such is not the case. The means of communicating with a large portion of the state are not in our power, and before the commencement of a Registration," he continued, "we ought to have undisputed control of a considerable territory, at least the two congressional districts proclaimed as not being in rebellion."[21]

Durant was aware when he posted his letter that Banks had tried to discredit him with the president, but he did not realize that someone else had also conspired against him. The pliant Michael Hahn, who was in Washington as one of the state's two "loyal" representatives, had decided to throw in with Banks.[22]

Between them, Banks and Hahn had systematically distorted what was happening in Louisiana in their reports to Lincoln. "The Union cause is going on gloriously here," Hahn had written to Lincoln after returning to the Crescent City for a visit in May. Banks gave the same optimistic account from Opelousas, where he was engaged in a campaign to penetrate the interior of the state. "It gives me pleasure to say to you that the sentiments of the people,

20. Cox, *Lincoln and Black Freedom*, 80; McCrary, *Lincoln and Reconstruction*, 209, 226–27; Tregle, "Thomas J. Durant," 502–6; Tunnell, *Crucible of Reconstruction*, 36–37, 42–43. Durant announced his support for limited black suffrage at a meeting of the Union National League at the Lyceum Hall on December 3, 1863 (*New Orleans Times*, December 4, 1863).

21. Cox, *Lincoln and Black Freedom*, 65; Tregle, "Thomas J. Durant," 506; Durant to Lincoln, October 1, 1863, Mounting No. 26839, Abraham Lincoln Papers, LC. According to McCrary (*Lincoln and Reconstruction*, 163), Durant's desire to have a substantial proportion of the electorate represented was not unrealistic. The thirteen parishes under Union control during the election for two congressional seats in December 1862 contained almost half of Louisiana's population. Tunnell reached the opposite conclusion by emphasizing how much of the state remained under Confederate control (Tunnell, *Crucible of Reconstruction*, 29).

22. McCrary, *Lincoln and Reconstruction*, 173; Tregle, "Thomas J. Durant," 507. Hahn had opposed secession but accepted a notary's post in the Confederate state government. After Butler occupied the city, Hahn quickly reasserted his pro-Union credentials (George S. Denison to Salmon P. Chase, February 19, 1864, in Salmon P. Chase, "Diary and Correspondence of Salmon P. Chase," *Annual Report of the American Historical Association; The Year 1902* [Washington, D.C.: U.S. Government Printing Office, 1903], 2:431).

are unexpectedly, and almost universally friendly to the restoration of the Government," he wrote. "Nothing is required but a sufficient force to hold the territory, to secure its immediate return to the Union."[23]

As a result of Banks's and Hahn's deception, Durant's letter came as a surprise to Lincoln. Lincoln had assumed that the registration of voters was proceeding smoothly. He was disappointed when he learned that it was not, for Lincoln needed a Unionist government in Louisiana quickly to demonstrate that he was winning the war.[24]

Lincoln fired off an angry letter to Banks on November 5. He had assumed that Durant "was taking a registry of citizens, preparatory to the election of a constitutional convention," the president began. "I now have his letter, written two months after . . . saying he is not taking registry; and he does not let me know that he personally is expecting to do so. This disappoints me bitterly," he continued, "yet I do not want to throw blame on you or them. I do however, urge both you and them, to lose no more time."[25]

Banks feigned bewilderment and hurt upon receiving Lincoln's letter. He did not realize, he wrote, that the president was counting on him to organize a new state government. Insinuating that Durant and Shepley had rejected his offer to help with the registration of voters, Banks noted that the military governor was in charge. "Had the organization of a *free* state in Louisiana been committed to me under general instructions only," he wrote, "it would have been complete before this day." Banks then promised to have everything ready within sixty days should Lincoln give him the authority to do so.[26]

Even before he received Banks's letter, Lincoln had decided to speed things along. In his annual address to Congress on December 9, the president announced a plan for the reconstruction of southern states. According to his plan, Lincoln would recognize the legitimacy of a state government as soon as it abolished slavery and reorganized itself on the basis of an election in which

23. Banks to Lincoln, May 4, 1863, and Hahn to Lincoln, May 9, 1863, Lincoln Papers; also see McCrary, *Lincoln and Reconstruction*, 105.

24. Cox, *Lincoln and Black Freedom*, 47.

25. Lincoln to Banks, November 5, 1863, in Basler, ed., *Collected Works of Abraham Lincoln*, 7:1–2.

26. Excerpts from Banks's letter to Lincoln, December 6, 1863, are in Basler, ed., *Collected Works of Abraham Lincoln*, 7:90–91; also see Cox, *Lincoln and Black Freedom*, 69. In *Crucible of Reconstruction* (p. 43) Tunnell opines that Banks was genuinely surprised when he received Lincoln's rebuke.

the number of voters who had taken an oath of loyalty exceeded 10 percent of the votes cast in the presidential election of 1860.[27]

Durant was ecstatic when he heard of the president's plan and urged Shepley to order an election. But it was Shepley who hesitated this time, caught between the Free State leader, Durant, and his military commander, Banks. Shepley decided on December 31 to ask Lincoln for permission to call for an election before proceeding. Informing the president that he was "anxious to conform to your views," Shepley asked to be reassured that what Durant proposed was in accord with the president's proclamation on reconstruction.[28]

Shepley's letter to the president crossed one in the mail from Lincoln to Banks. Frustrated by the slow pace of reconstruction in Louisiana and believing Banks's claim that he could get things done, Lincoln wrote the Massachusetts politician on Christmas Eve, apologizing for having wounded Banks's feelings and giving him absolute authority to direct the effort to reconstruct Louisiana. "Give us a free-state organization of Louisiana in the shortest possible time," Lincoln urged.[29]

Using his newfound authority, Banks acted swiftly. On January 11, 1864, he issued a proclamation ordering an election on February 22 for governor, lieutenant governor, and several other state offices. Any white male who took an oath of loyalty to the Constitution, laws, and president of the United States would be allowed to vote. In addition, Banks announced that there would be an election on March 28 for delegates to a constitutional convention. In the meantime, the state would continue to operate under its constitution of 1852, stripped of its provisions relating to slavery.[30]

Durant was deeply disappointed at Lincoln's decision to place absolute

27. Lincoln, "Proclamation," December 8, 1863, in Basler, ed., *Collected Works of Abraham Lincoln*, 7:55; McCrary, *Lincoln and Reconstruction*, 186–91. Fifty thousand votes were cast in the 1860 presidential election in Louisiana (Vandal, "New Orleans Riot," 18).

28. Shepley to Lincoln, December 31, 1863, Mounting No. 29036, Lincoln Papers; also see McCrary, *Lincoln and Reconstruction*, 195–99.

29. Lincoln to Banks, December 24, 1863, in Basler, ed., *Collected Works of Abraham Lincoln*, 7:89–90; also see Cox, *Lincoln and Black Freedom*, 62–63; Tunnell, *Crucible of Reconstruction*, 48.

30. "The Qualifications of Electors," *New Orleans Daily True Delta*, February 21, 1864. Banks's proclamation, "To the People of Louisiana" (January 11, 1864), appeared in several papers, including his own, the *New Orleans Era*. Also see *OR*, Ser. III, 4: 22–23; Ripley, *Slaves and Freedmen*, 162-63; Vandal, "New Orleans Riot," 7; and Cox, *Lincoln and Black Freedom*, 58. McCrary (*Lincoln and Reconstruction*, 207) suggests that Banks ordered the election for state offices first because it would be easier for him to organize a slate of six or seven candidates for state offices than to orchestrate the election of almost a hundred convention delegates.

power regarding the future of Louisiana in the hands of an opportunistic politician. Accordingly, Durant resigned as attorney general so that he could oppose Banks openly without being accused of disloyalty.[31]

Durant's defection widened a split among Unionists that had been in the making since Banks's arrival. The primary issue was race. Conservative Unionists wanted blacks to remain in a posture of perpetual subservience. Radical Unionists under the leadership of Durant favored the inclusion of blacks in the mainstream of society, which included giving some blacks, particularly those who had been free before the war, the right to vote. A third faction of Unionists adhered to a position that fell between those of the conservatives and the Radicals. Unlike the conservatives, they were not opposed to granting blacks their civil rights, but they disagreed with the Radicals over how quickly the rehabilitation of former slaves should proceed. The Radicals wanted change now; the faction in between thought that it should proceed at a slower pace. They wanted to pursue a gradual program of social change that would not alienate the majority of white Louisianians. The Radicals believed that most whites in Louisiana would never voluntarily accede to the quest for black civil rights, regardless of the pace at which it occurred.[32]

The extent to which the three sides disagreed became apparent on February 1, 1864, when the state's Unionists convened in New Orleans to nominate candidates for the upcoming elections. After a bitter debate over the credentials of delegates from several rural parishes, the Radicals pulled out, leaving the delegates who favored gradual change in control. They nominated Michael Hahn, the young lawyer who had been sent to Washington in 1862 to represent Louisiana, for governor. In a separate meeting, the Radicals named Benjamin F. Flanders, the other congressional delegate, as their candidate. Pleased by the falling-out between the gradualists and the Radicals, conservative Unionists put forth the name of a well-to-do New Orleans lawyer, J. Q. A. Fellows.[33]

Black suffrage quickly emerged as the central issue in the campaign for

31. Durant to Lincoln, February 26, 1864, Lincoln Papers; Durant to Shepley, January 13, 1864, Thomas J. Durant Papers, NYHS; McCrary, *Lincoln and Reconstruction*, 186; Ripley, *Slaves and Freedmen*, 167; Tunnell, *Crucible of Reconstruction*, 30.

32. Cox, *Lincoln and Black Freedom*, 75–76, 81; McCrary, *Lincoln and Reconstruction*, 208, 226–27, 349; Mark W. Summers, "The Moderates' Last Chance: The Louisiana Election of 1865," *Louisiana History* 24 (Winter 1983): 50–54; Tunnell, *Crucible of Reconstruction*, 5, 38–39, 41, 60.

33. *New Orleans Daily True Delta*, February 2, 1864; *New Orleans Era*, February 2, 1864; Cox, *Lincoln and Black Freedom*, 86; McCrary, *Lincoln and Reconstruction*, 218–23.

governor. Hahn straddled the issue. "While he (Flanders) believes that the right of suffrage should be extended to the negroes," the *Era* reported after the splintered convention, "Mr. Hahn believes that the time has not yet arrived." Flanders attempted to defuse the issue by stating that although he favored emancipation, he "had never advocated" giving blacks the vote; he "did not deem it practicable."[34]

Banks threw his support behind Hahn and worked hard to ensure a large turnout. He ordered regimental bands to provide music at Hahn rallies and made election day a holiday. He directed Louisianians serving in Union regiments to cast ballots, although in some cases soldiers who were residents of other states ended up voting. Banks also allowed Unionists who had fled from areas under Confederate control to cast their ballots in New Orleans. Much to his satisfaction, eleven thousand voters went to the polls on Washington's birthday, February 22, making the turnout twice the size required to satisfy Lincoln's 10 percent stipulation. Not surprisingly, Hahn won by a wide margin over his two opponents, Flanders and Fellows.[35]

Michael Hahn was sworn in as the first governor of the Free State of Louisiana on March 4, 1864, amid a parade with floats, banners, fireworks, and the music of three hundred musicians aided by an anvil chorus of forty more. A choir of schoolchildren from the New Orleans public schools sang to the crowd of twenty thousand in Lafayette Square. Edward H. Durell, recently confirmed by the U.S. Senate as district court judge for eastern Louisiana, administered the oath of office to the new governor. Banks was ecstatic. He had "never witnessed such a spectacle elsewhere," he wrote in his report. There was "no sounder basis for a State government in this country."[36]

Not everyone agreed with Banks's assessment. "This election does not restore Louisiana to the Union," Durant contended. The new state officers are

34. *New Orleans Daily True Delta*, February 12, 21, 1864; *New Orleans Era*, February 1, 9, 1864; *New Orleans Times*, February 20, 1864; Cox, *Lincoln and Black Freedom*, 89, 91; McCrary, *Lincoln and Reconstruction*, 212, 226.

35. *New Orleans Era*, January 29, 1864; Cox, *Lincoln and Black Freedom*, 108; Harrington, *Fighting Politician*, 144; McCrary, *Lincoln and Reconstruction*, 208, 234, 240; Ripley, *Slaves and Freedmen*, 170. The vote was 6,183 for Hahn, 2,996 for Fellows, and 2,322 for Flanders (*New Orleans Daily True Delta*, February 23, 1864; for additional returns, see *OR*, Ser. III, 4:134–35).

36. *New Orleans Times*, March 5, 1864; *New Orleans Daily Picayune*, March 5, 1864; Banks to Halleck, March 6, 1864, *OR*, 34: pt. 2, 512–13; also see Banks to Lincoln, February 25, 1864, *OR*, Ser. III, 4:133–34; Banks to William Lloyd Garrison, January 30, 1865, printed in the *Liberator*, February 24, 1865; Thomas W. Helis, "Of Generals and Jurists: The Judicial System of New Orleans Under Union Occupation, May 1862–April 1865," *Louisiana History* 29 (Spring 1988): 158.

"but the fragment of government." Henry Winter Davis, a congressman with a Radical bent, criticized Lincoln for having given Banks the power to interfere with the electoral process. Lincoln "has called on General Banks to organize another hermaphrodite government," Davis proclaimed in a speech on the House floor, "half military and half republican, representing the alligators and frogs of Louisiana."[37]

Despite these criticisms, Banks went ahead with his plans to hold an election for delegates to a constitutional convention. Although friends urged Durant to run as a delegate, the independent lawyer decided to continue his boycott of anything that had to do with Nathaniel P. Banks. Banks "is now about to declare how many members shall be elected to a constitutional convention, what shall be the basis of representation, and what the details of the election [will be]," Durant wrote Secretary of the Treasury Salmon P. Chase on the day after Hahn's inauguration, "which simply means that he will declare who the members of the convention shall be and what the convention shall do." Durant planned to ask his supporters in the U.S. Congress to block the recognition of Banks's puppet regime.[38]

Once again, free blacks in New Orleans had beaten Durant to the punch. Eight days after Banks issued his proclamation calling for elections, free men of color had held another mass meeting to select two delegates to represent their interests in Washington. The two men they selected, Jean Baptiste Roudanez (an engineer) and Arnold Bertonneau (a wine merchant), were well-educated, prominent businessmen. Bertonneau had also served as an officer in the Louisiana Native Guards. Leaving New Orleans in mid-February, they met with Lincoln in his office on March 12 and delivered a petition signed by a thousand of their free black compatriots. The president remained noncommittal during the meeting, but he was impressed. The next day Lincoln composed a confidential letter to Michael Hahn. "I barely suggest, for your private consideration," he wrote, "whether some of the colored people may not be let in, as, for instance, the very intelligent, and especially those who have fought gallantly in our ranks." Although Hahn waited more than two years before releasing the contents of the letter, the die had been cast. Hahn had been

37. Durant to Henry Winter Davis, March 31, 1864, Durant Papers; Durant to Lincoln, February 26, 1864, Lincoln Papers; *Congressional Globe*, 38th Cong., 1st sess. (February 16, 1864), 680–82.

38. *New Orleans Times*, March 19, 1864; Durant to Chase, March 5, 1864, Salmon P. Chase Papers, LC; Cox, *Lincoln and Black Freedom*, 92–93; McCrary, *Lincoln and Reconstruction*, 239, 241. A devastating indictment of the Free State can be found in *Some Remarks upon the Proposed Election of February 22d* (New Orleans[?]: N.p., 1864[?]).

nudged toward the Radical side, and Banks, always eager to strengthen his ties to Lincoln, decided that suffrage limited to black men who had been free before the war was not so bad after all.[39]

Unaware that Lincoln had written Hahn in support of limited black suffrage, Trévigne did not wait for Roudanez and Bertonneau to return before demanding universal male suffrage. The qualification to vote should be based on "the rightful capacity of all native and free born Americans by virtue of their nativity in the country, irrespective of national descent, wealth or intelligence," Trévigne argued in *L'Union*, "and that all not free, within the state, be immediately enfranchised by the abolition of slavery in the state forever, and by a statute or constitutional provision declaring the absolute equality of all free men as to their governmental rights."[40]

The election for delegates to the constitutional convention occurred as scheduled on March 28, 1864. The day was cold and rainy, and the turnout was low. Nevertheless, ninety-five delegates were elected. They represented "the heart of the people," Banks told Lincoln. That may have been true, but not very many people had elected them. Because the Radicals had boycotted the election and because the conservatives were off fighting for the Confederacy, most of the delegates were supporters of Michael Hahn. Only Edmund Abell, a conservative lawyer from the Fifth District, and three other delegates had not run on the Hahn ticket. Furthermore, few of the delegates resided outside of New Orleans. Just as Durant had predicted, the constitutional convention of 1864 was a partisan body elected to strengthen Banks's political base.[41]

39. "President Lincoln's Letter to Gov. Hahn," *New Orleans Daily Picayune*, July 6, 1865; Hollandsworth, *Louisiana Native Guards*, 3, 73, 94–95; Logsdon and Bell, "Americanization of Black New Orleans," 224-26; McCrary, *Lincoln and Reconstruction*, 229, 254–55; Ripley, *Slaves and Freedmen*, 164; Tunnell, *Crucible of Reconstruction*, 39, 78–79.

40. *L'Union* quotation from Logsdon and Bell, "Americanization of Black New Orleans," 228.

41. "The New Orleans Horror," *Chicago Tribune*, August 8, 1866; Banks to Mary Banks, April 2, 1863, Banks Collection; *OR*, 34: pt. 1, 179–80, Ser. III, 4:170–72, 209; McCrary, *Lincoln and Reconstruction*, 244; Vandal, "New Orleans Riot," 42–43. Although Banks opened the polls in Opelousas, Marksville, Harrisonburg, and Alexandria during his excursion up the Red River in April 1864, the turnout was light.

2

No Better Constitution

ELEGATES to the constitutional convention began their work in New Orleans on April 6, 1864, and met for the next four months. They were not men who were bent on radically changing their world. Far from being revolutionaries, they were drawn mostly from the state's middle class: lawyers, medical doctors, educators, and businessmen with a few farmers, shopkeepers, and artisans thrown in. With the exception of two delegates who were sons of Unionist planters, the planter elite, which had run the state before the war, was absent.[1]

On April 7, the delegates elected Judge Edmund H. Durell president over his opponent, Judge Rufus K. Howell, by a vote of forty-three to forty-one. After adopting rules and regulations under which to operate and dividing the delegates among eighteen standing committees, the convention was ready to begin its deliberation.[2]

1. *DCCL*, 300–301; John G. Nicolay and John Hay, *Abraham Lincoln: A History*, 10 vols. (New York: Century, 1914), 8: 435–36; Vandal, "New Orleans Riot," 43–44. For a thorough analysis of the convention's membership, see McCrary, *Lincoln and Reconstruction*, 245–52, 371–72. See Tunnell, *Crucible of Reconstruction*, 56–59, for an analysis of convention membership that emphasizes the Radical faction.

2. *DCCL*, 6–7, 22–25, 43–44. Durell was the son of a distinguished New Hampshire jurist and graduated from Phillips Exeter and Harvard. After reading law in his father's office, he was

Confederate sympathizers in New Orleans were quick to brand the delegates as inept opportunists, or "carpetbaggers," because many of them had been born in the North. Northern nativity, however, was not unusual in the Crescent City. In fact, many of its most distinguished citizens, particularly in business and the professions, had emigrated to New Orleans to seek their fortunes. But one would be hard-pressed to say that the convention was composed of carpetbaggers. All of the non-native delegates, with one exception, had resided in Louisiana for many years.[3]

Black Louisianians and white Radicals were skeptical of the delegates' intentions as well. Blacks doubted whether the delegates had any interest in drafting a new constitution for Louisiana that would recognize the rights and needs of those citizens who until recently had been bought and sold as property, and white Radicals believed that the delegates were more interested in promoting their own interests than mending a broken society based on slavery.[4]

Delegates to the constitutional convention promptly validated pessimistic assessments of their selfish intentions by voting themselves a generous per diem and by running up extravagant expenditures for food and liquor. "In the public estimation," treasury agent George S. Denison wrote to Secretary Salmon P. Chase, "General Banks' State Convention stands no higher than Banks himself. 'What fools they are making of themselves' is a very common remark, even among those who helped elect them."[5]

Fools or not, the delegates had serious work cut out for them. The paramount issue facing the body was the abolition of slavery. Because it applied

---

admitted to the bar in 1834 and set up practice in New Orleans shortly thereafter (McCrary, *Lincoln and Reconstruction*, 250).

3. McCrary, *Lincoln and Reconstruction*, 246; Tunnell, *Crucible of Reconstruction*, 20, 27. Traditional historiography regarding Reconstruction (i.e., the Dunning school) depicted the delegates as "among the most rabid of the radicals and typical carpetbaggers in every sense of the term" (Francis P. Burns, "White Supremacy in the South: The Battle for Constitutional Government in New Orleans, July 30, 1866," *Louisiana Historical Quarterly* 18 [July 1935], 596–97). Vandal's thorough analysis of the convention's membership has completely discredited this view. The exception to a lengthy residency in Louisiana before the convention was "Colonel" Alfred C. Hills.

4. McCrary, *Lincoln and Reconstruction*, 241–42; Ripley, *Slaves and Freedmen*, 171; Tunnell, *Crucible of Reconstruction*, 49–50.

5. George S. Denison to Salmon P. Chase, June 17, 1864, in Chase, "Diary and Correspondence," 2:439. Most New Orleanians dismissed the convention as a "mere sham" (*HSCR*, 221). For an analysis of the convention's many fiscal improprieties, see Vandal, "New Orleans Riot," 48–52.

only to those parts of the country still in rebellion, Lincoln's Emancipation Proclamation had not freed slaves in areas of Louisiana that were occupied by Union troops at the time it went into effect. Thus slave owners in New Orleans and southeastern Louisiana who could prove their loyalty were entitled to keep their slaves.

The Committee on Emancipation presented its report on April 27. The report contained five sections. The first section abolished slavery and involuntary servitude, except as punishment for a crime. The second section precluded the legislature from making any law recognizing "the right of property in man." The third section annulled the antebellum Black Code, and the fourth guaranteed equal treatment before the law regardless of race. The final section provided for indentured minors as apprentices but prescribed that those laws should affect minors of African descent on the same terms and conditions as applied to whites.[6]

None of the delegates to the convention expected that slavery would survive the war, but they needed to address the issue of compensation for slave owners. Edmund Abell, a forty-four-year-old Kentucky-born lawyer who had lived in New Orleans since 1847, filed a minority report that proposed delaying emancipation until the legislature and the federal government could develop a plan by which to pay all loyal owners for their slave property. In addition, Abell's report called for the removal of all former slaves from the state so that they could not compete with white labor on the free market.[7]

In reality, Abell was opposed to emancipation regardless of whether the slave owner was compensated. Although he was a staunch Union man, Abell's sympathies lay with the slaveholders, which became obvious when he took the floor on May 3 to debate the committee's report. "The negroes, when they are in slavery, have homes where they are cared for and protected," Abell noted. "Make them free, and they will be driven out upon the world, a most miserable, outcast, homeless set—the most wretched people on the face of the earth. At home in slavery they are—with the exception of those under cruel masters, and God knows I detest a cruel master from the bottom of my heart—a happy, contented people." Reflecting the assumptions held by most southern whites at the time, Abell reiterated his point: "I say that of all systems of labor, slavery

6. *DCCL*, 69–76, 96.
7. *DCCL*, 97–98; William Russell Abell, "Judge Edmund Abell and the New Orleans Riots of 1866" (Des Moines, Iowa, 1986, typescript in New Orleans Public Library), 1, 4. Abell was among the most conservative of the convention delegates (see Table C-4 in McCrary, *Abraham Lincoln and Reconstruction*, 378–79).

is the most perfect, humane, and satisfactory that has ever been devised; and a slave under a good master is the most happy being in the world."[8]

R. King Cutler, a forty-seven-year-old midwesterner who had lived in New Orleans for almost thirty years, rose to respond to Abell's argument. "I am not in favor of emancipating them because their condition is at this moment better off in Dixie; nor of keeping them in bondage because they are better off as slaves," Cutler announced, "but because of the fact that we have a great rebellion in our midst, and it is necessary, in the opinion of the Government and people, to do so in order to put down this rebellion." Cutler did not want to seem too radical. "I am not one of those abolitionists who desires the emancipation simply because it is a great good to humanity," he continued, "nor am I here to discuss whether a state of slavery or a state of freedom is most beneficial to the negro. I leave that to some other time, as the question does not necessarily arise now; but I do say that slaves in every State of this rebellious country should be set at liberty for the purpose of crushing this odious rebellion. [Applause.]"[9]

Cutler's argument was persuasive. Abell tried to do what he could to delay a vote on the committee's report. At the very least, loyal slave owners should be compensated for their loss, he argued. Pointing out that the majority report "proposes at one single swoop to dispossess owners of their property," Abell urged each delegate "to ask himself the question, is this right, is it fair, is it honest? Is it acting upon the great principle that requires you to do to others as you would that they should do to you?"[10]

John Henderson, Cutler's law partner, responded to Abell's question. "Slavery is both contrary to the law of nations and natural law," Henderson proclaimed. "If you carry a negro into England or Ireland, his shackles fall off; but yet if he chooses to go back to the land of his birth, they may be riveted on him again. Beautiful consistency!" Like Cutler before him, Henderson tied emancipation to the war effort. "I was willing some four years ago to abolish slavery gradually," he continued, "and would have voted to do so; but I was as from a dream, and find this great republican master spirit of the world demands the abolition of it now, in order to save the Union. So I say down with it! [Applause.]"[11]

---

8. May 3, 1864, *DCCL*, 155–56.

9. *DCCL*, 160–61; Glen R. Conrad, ed., *A Dictionary of Louisiana Biography*, 2 vols. (New Orleans: Louisiana Historical Association in cooperation with the Center for Louisiana Studies, 1988), 1:206.

10. *DCCL*, 166. A motion to take up the committee report and consider it until it was "finally disposed of" passed by a vote of fifty-four to twenty-six on May 4 (*DCCL*, 163).

11. *DCCL*, 170; McCrary, *Lincoln and Reconstruction*, 250.

Abell would not give up. Thursday, Friday, and Saturday the debate continued. Abell and several other conservative delegates tried to persuade the convention to make emancipation contingent on federal compensation of loyal slaveholders. If successful, the motion would have postponed the abolition of slavery indefinitely. Finally, the delegates in favor of uncompensated emancipation succeeded in tabling Abell's proposal.[12]

Abell and his allies were not about to give up. The next day, Abell attached an amendment to the third section of the committee's report, the section that abolished the antebellum slave code. Abell could support the abolishment of the black codes, he declared, "provided, always, that the Legislature shall never pass any act authorizing free negroes to vote." Abell's interjection of the suffrage issue was tactically sound, for whatever the opinion of the white delegates regarding the institution of slavery, few of them were willing to endorse the right of black men, free or former slave, to vote. By an overwhelming majority of seventy-five to fifteen, the convention passed Abell's amendment.[13]

Delegates in favor of uncompensated emancipation regrouped under the leadership of Cyrus W. Stauffer and countered the conservatives the following day. With a bold stroke, Stauffer moved that the entire third section be struck from the report. Stauffer's motion garnered conservative support, for although it voided Abell's amendment regarding suffrage, it also removed the prohibition against the Black Code. Another delegate gained the floor and offered to strike sections four and five, those dealing with equal treatment before the law and indentured minors, as part of Stauffer's amendment. Stauffer accepted the additions, and the expanded motion passed by a vote of fifty-nine to thirty-two.[14]

The Emancipation Committee's report now included only two sections. The first abolished slavery and involuntary servitude except as punishment for a crime. The second prohibited the legislature from making any law recognizing "the right of property in man." Sensing that momentum was in their favor, a delegate who supported uncompensated emancipation moved to suspend the rules and bring the article to a final vote. Despite Abell's vigorous opposition, the measure passed by a vote of seventy-two to thirteen. When President Durell announced the outcome, the chamber exploded with enthusiastic cheers.

12. *DCCL*, 206–8.

13. *DCCL*, 211–12. The vote on May 10 was sixty-eight in favor, fifteen opposed. Eight delegates recorded their votes in favor of Abell's amendment when the convention resumed business the following day (ibid., 218–19).

14. *DCCL*, 221–22.

Slavery would be dead everywhere in Louisiana once the document was ratified.[15]

The issue of black suffrage came before the convention when the Committee on the Legislative Department issued its report on May 17. This report limited the right to vote to white males twenty-one years of age or older who had been residents in the state of Louisiana for at least twelve months, who were citizens of the United States, and who were able to read and write. But it also contained a significant loophole by providing that "the legislature shall have power to pass laws extending suffrage to such other persons, citizens of the United States, as by military service, by taxation to support the government, or by intellectual fitness, may be deemed entitled thereto."[16]

The provision referred to men of color who had been free before the war, many of whom had served in the United States Army. Its inclusion should not have been surprising, for the free black community had been calling for the right to vote for almost a year, and even Banks had finally embraced the concept of limited black suffrage. But a majority of the delegates were not willing to give black men the vote, regardless of their qualifications. As soon as the Legislative Committee submitted its report, a conservative delegate moved to strike an article that would allow the legislature to enfranchise black males. The motion carried by a vote of fifty-three to twenty-three.[17]

For the time being, the issue was dead, but delegates who favored black suffrage in some form were not finished. Turning to General Banks and Governor Hahn, they sought to bring pressure on delegates to change their votes. For the next two months, as the convention turned its attention to other matters, Banks and Hahn used promises of elected offices and well-paying government positions to induce reluctant delegates to allow the legislature to enfranchise "such other persons" who "may be deemed entitled thereto."[18]

By mid-June, delegates in favor of limited black suffrage had the votes they needed. Their biggest obstacle was Judge Abell, who might use his parliamen-

15. *DCCL*, 223–24.

16. *DCCL*, 237, 244. A person also had to reside in the parish where he planned to vote for at least six months.

17. *DCCL*, 249–50; McCrary, *Lincoln and Reconstruction*, 254–64; Tunnell, *Crucible of Reconstruction*, 40.

18. George S. Denison to Salmon P. Chase, October 8, November 25, 1864, in Chase, "Diary and Correspondence," 2:449–55; Cox, *Lincoln and Black Freedom*, 98; Tunnell, *Crucible of Reconstruction*, 41–42, 63–64; Vandal, "New Orleans Riot," 48–49, 72. Banks had urged Judge Durell to extend suffrage to blacks on the basis of intelligence and taxation even before the convention convened.

tary skill to delay a vote on the measure, which would allow the conservatives time to regroup, or whose outspoken opposition might sway some delegates at the last minute to the conservative side. Fortunately for the delegates who favored limited black suffrage, a narrow window of opportunity presented itself on June 23.

The session opened with the usual business of debating and approving general provisions to the constitution. Abell answered the roll call but left the hall when the delegates began debating a motion to prevent foreigners from engaging in professions, occupations, or businesses requiring a license. The reason for Abell's absence may have been his desire to confer with Banks on the matter of compensation for loyal slave owners. It is even possible that Banks had agreed to lure Abell away from the session so that the motion could be rushed through. Whatever the case, after the antiforeigner motion had been defeated and another article dealing with the state poorhouse tabled, Joseph Gorlinski, a Polish immigrant, reintroduced the article that would allow the legislature to extend the right to vote "to such persons, citizens of the United States," who had demonstrated their capacity for participation in the affairs of government by military service, taxation, or intellectual fitness.[19]

John Sullivan, a delegate from New Orleans and night watchman at the U.S. Custom House, rose to object. "I move to lay it on the table," he shouted. "That's a nigger resolution." But the delegates in favor of limited black suffrage were well prepared, and Abell's absence left the conservative forces momentarily in disarray. Durell called for a voice vote and declared that the article had been rejected. The prosuffrage delegates demanded a roll call, and the article passed by a vote of forty-eight to thirty-two. Abell returned minutes later, but it was too late.[20] The compromise, which let the legislature decide on the issue of black suffrage, had become part of the Louisiana constitution.

The convention continued its work for another month before finalizing the new constitution on July 22. The document was essentially a revised and amended copy of Louisiana's constitution of 1852, but it did contain some notable provisions. For one, it abolished slavery. It also established segregated public schools for black and white children and increased the income of New Orleans workingmen by setting minimum wages for public employment.[21]

Sixty-six delegates voted to adopt the constitution. Sixteen, including Judge Abell, voted against it. Nevertheless, Louisiana now had a constitution

---

19. McCrary, *Lincoln and Reconstruction*, 263, n. 64; *DCCL*, 446–47, 450.
20. McCrary, *Lincoln and Reconstruction*, 247; *DCCL*, 450–51.
21. McCrary, *Lincoln and Reconstruction*, 259–60.

that abolished slavery, which was a prerequisite under the conditions of Lincoln's 10 percent plan for gaining readmission to the Union. But the question of black suffrage, which had been left to the legislature, was far from being settled.[22]

Expecting something more than the tentative promise of suffrage in the future, free blacks in New Orleans expressed their disgust with the new constitution in the *New Orleans Tribune*, which had replaced *L'Union* as the voice of the free black community. Instead of embracing black suffrage as "an example of liberty . . . that other free states could emulate for the elevation of the black race," the editor of the *Tribune*, complained, "some of our best and wisest men" had actually moved further away from the idea. The problem, according to the *Tribune*, was "the deep-rooted prejudice against this people [that] still remains in all its pristine vigor, in the North as much as the South, and will so continue till public opinion shall be brought up to a higher standard and recognizes the true principle of politics that, before the law all men are equal."[23]

Ignoring the growing dissatisfaction in the free black community, Banks threw his influence and prestige behind the ratification of the new document. He admonished Louisiana citizens in federal uniforms to cast their ballots, reminding them that "a citizen who refuses to support his government with musket or ballot has but slender claims for its favor or protection." He reminded laborers on public works that they depended on the state government for their pay and informed workingmen in general of the clauses in the constitution that would benefit them. Governor Hahn and many of his state officials also pitched in to get out the vote. In addition, Lincoln lent his support by letting it be known that he approved of the document. It is "excellent," Lincoln said, "better for the poor black than [the one] we have in Illinois."[24]

Despite a low turnout, the constitution was ratified by a vote of more than

22. *DCCL*, 607, 643.

23. *New Orleans Tribune*, July 28, August 11, 1864; see also Tunnell, *Crucible of Reconstruction*, 79. *L'Union* folded on July 19, 1864, because of money problems. Dr. Louis Charles Roudanez, a physician who had attended medical school in Paris, threw his financial support behind a new venture, the *New Orleans Tribune*, edited by Paul Trévigne from *L'Union*. Dr. Louis Roudanez was the brother of Jean Baptiste Roudanez, one of the two emissaries from the free black community who had met with Lincoln in March (Connor, "Reconstruction Rebels," 160–63; Logsdon and Bell, "Americanization of Black New Orleans," 229).

24. Cox, *Lincoln and Black Freedom*, 102; Harrington, *Fighting Politician*, 149; Ripley, *Slaves and Freedmen*, 176–77; Lincoln to Banks, April 11, 1865, in Nicolay and Hay, *Abraham Lincoln*, 8:435–36; Lincoln to Banks, August 9, 1864, Banks to Joseph Both, September 4, 1864 (printed circular), Banks Collection.

four to one on September 5, 1864.²⁵ Elections for the legislature, which were held on the same day, drew greater interest. Nevertheless, the Free State constitution had been adopted. It was "one of the best ever penned," Banks proclaimed with his usual hyperbole. "No better constitution has ever been presented to any people on the face of the earth, and there never will be till the end of time." If the U.S. Congress accepted his plan for reconstructing the southern states, Banks predicted, all the problems associated with reuniting the country after the war would be solved.²⁶

25. The vote was 6,836 in favor of ratification and 1,566 against (McCrary, *Lincoln and Reconstruction*, 269).

26. *Boston Daily Journal*, November 1, 1864; Banks to Mary Banks, August 31, September 6, 1864, October 20, 1871, Lincoln to Banks, August 9, 1864, Banks Collection. Although the new constitution may not have been the best "ever . . . presented to any people on the face of the earth," it was certainly a better document than the Dunning school of Reconstruction has claimed. For an example of a more recent revisionist view, see Cox, *Lincoln and Black Freedom*, 102–3.

3

There Is No Middle Ground

T HE FREE STATE of Louisiana had a rough time of it from the start. Not surprisingly, attacks came from both the conservatives and the Radicals. Founded by men who believed that changes initiated by four years of civil war should be implemented gradually and be limited in their scope, the Free State was destined to disappoint everyone who held strong opinions about what Louisiana should be like in the future.

Banks's old foe Thomas J. Durant led the Radical assault. While the constitutional convention was hammering out the provisions of a new charter in the midsummer heat of New Orleans, Durant traveled to Washington to lobby against recognition of the Free State of Louisiana.[1]

Durant found a receptive audience among key Republican leaders in Congress, notably Representative Henry Winter Davis and Senator Benjamin F. Wade. Both men were opposed to Lincoln's plan for Reconstruction. Although they liked the aspect of the president's plan that required states to ac-

1. Belz, *Reconstructing the Union*, 192–93; McCrary, *Lincoln and Reconstruction*, 232, 285. Durant's biographer, Joseph Tregle, stated, "Probably no man [Durant] did so much to convince Congress and a broad segment of the American public that Presidential Reconstruction, at least in Louisiana, was a betrayal of the cause of freedom and American republicanism" ("Thomas J. Durant," 511).

cept emancipation as a condition for readmission, they believed that the president was too lenient when he promised a pardon for any Confederate who took an oath of loyalty. In addition, the Radicals were displeased over a provision in Lincoln's plan that upheld the qualifications for voters in effect at the time of secession. Such a provision would ensure that blacks would be prevented from voting.[2]

Under the leadership of Wade and Davis, opponents of the Free State of Louisiana developed their own plan for Reconstruction. Introduced during the summer of 1864, the Wade-Davis Bill called for the registration of all white male citizens in each southern state. After a majority, not 10 percent, of registered voters took an oath of allegiance to the Constitution of the United States, a new state government could be organized. No one who had voluntarily fought for the Confederacy or who had held office in the Confederate government would be allowed to vote.[3]

Lincoln realized that the bill's requirements were so stringent that it would effectively postpone the readmission of the southern states until after the war was over. Consequently, he refused to sign the measure when it came to his desk in July 1864. Angered by the rejection of their proposal, supporters of the Wade-Davis Bill swore to block the president's design for Reconstruction.[4]

Hoping to forestall the growing opposition to their fledgling government, members of the Free State legislature assembled in October to elect two senators for the posts vacated in 1861 when Louisiana seceded. Michael Hahn was named to one, and R. King Cutler was given the other. Not realizing that he would be prevented from taking his seat because of opposition in Congress, Hahn resigned as governor and handed the reins of government to the lieutenant governor, J. Madison Wells.[5]

2. Lincoln, "Proclamation," December 8, 1863, in Basler, ed., *Collected Works of Abraham Lincoln*, 7:55; Belz, *Reconstructing the Union*, 155–67, 183; McCrary, *Lincoln and Reconstruction*, 189–91, 233; James M. McPherson, *The Struggle for Equality: Abolitionists and the Negro in the Civil War and Reconstruction* (Princeton, N.J.: Princeton University Press, 1964), 245–46.

3. Belz, *Reconstructing the Union*, 168, 198–208, 210–11; Ripley, *Slaves and Freedmen*, 176.

4. Belz, *Reconstructing the Union*, 189–90, 223–28, 271; McCrary, *Lincoln and Reconstruction*, 275–77, 290–304. The Radicals were successful. Although there was widespread support in the Senate for recognizing the Free State of Louisiana, Charles Sumner was able to keep it from coming to a vote by threatening a filibuster (David Donald, *Charles Sumner and the Rights of Man* [New York: Knopf, 1970], 203–5).

5. *New Orleans Daily Picayune*, February 28, 1865; *New Orleans Era*, March 8, 10, October 11, 1864. The legislature also considered two bills granting limited suffrage for blacks, but they were soundly defeated despite Governor Hahn's support (Vandal, "New Orleans Riot," 60). Hahn submitted his resignation on February 27, effective March 3, 1864. Wells was born in 1808 (Tunnell, *Crucible of Reconstruction*, 22).

Wells had a curious political history. Both the gradualists and the Radicals had nominated him in 1864 for lieutenant governor, and he had beaten his conservative opponent easily. But Wells turned his back on those who endorsed him and tied in with the conservatives once he became governor in March 1865.[6]

The conversion was not as strange as it first appeared, for the fifty-eight-year-old Wells was a native-born Louisiana planter, a member of the old slaveholding aristocracy. He never did fit into the Banks-Hahn faction that drew its support from white workingmen and middle-class professionals, nor did he feel at home with the Radicals, who advocated black suffrage. His nomination as lieutenant governor had been designed to draw votes from Louisiana's planter class, and he realigned himself with that constituency as soon as he became governor.[7]

Once in office, the normally quiet Wells went on the offensive. He fired Banks's old friend and political ally Stephen Hoyt as mayor of New Orleans and replaced him with a conservative newspaper editor, Hugh Kennedy. Wells also removed Banks's registrar of voters, J. Randall Terry, and declared that Terry's voter rolls were null and void. So it went throughout the various administrative departments of the city as Wells replaced pro-Banks men with his supporters.[8]

Wells made these changes while Banks was in Washington consulting with Lincoln. When Banks returned to New Orleans in April 1865, he used his military authority to dismiss Mayor Kennedy and named his own man, Samuel M. Quincy, as acting mayor. Quincy quickly reestablished control over the

6. A. P. Field to Banks, November 20, 1865, Banks Collection; T. P. May to Maj. Gen. Carl Schurz, September 6, 1865, Michael Hahn to Schurz, September 6, 1865, both in Carl Schurz Papers, LC; McCrary, *Lincoln and Reconstruction*, 308.

7. McCrary, *Lincoln and Reconstruction*, 240–41; Ripley, *Slaves and Freedmen*, 182–83; Tunnell, *Crucible of Reconstruction*, 95–99; Vandal, "New Orleans Riot," 40–44. For evidence of the Banks-Hahn ties to labor, see Charles Smith's speech, *New Orleans Daily True Delta*, November 6, 1864, and campaign slogans printed in the *New Orleans Daily True Delta*, February 13, 1864.

8. Walter M. Lowrey, "The Political Career of James Madison Wells," *Louisiana Historical Quarterly* 31 (October 1948): 1028–30; Emily Hazen Reed, *Life of A. P. Dostie; or, The Conflict in New Orleans* (New York: Wm. P. Tomlinson, 1868), 181–83, 190–92; *New Orleans Daily Picayune*, March 29, April 9, May 9, 1865; *New Orleans Daily True Delta*, May 11, 1865; *New Orleans Tribune*, May 12, 1865. For Kennedy's reputation as a slavery advocate, see George S. Denison to Salmon P. Chase, May 9, 1863, March 21, 1865, in Chase, "Diary and Correspondence," 2:387, 457; see also McCrary, *Lincoln and Reconstruction*, 310–11; Ripley, *Slaves and Freedmen*, 183; Summers, "Moderates' Last Chance," 54–55; Tunnell, *Crucible of Reconstruction*, 96; Vandal, "New Orleans Riot," 80.

municipal machine, and supporters of the Free State regime flocked to the jobs that they had recently lost. Although Wells fought back by telling the city treasurer not to honor warrants drawn by the new mayor, Quincy held the upper hand as long as he was supported by Union bayonets.[9]

Support for Quincy's regime was short-lived, however, for an assassin's bullet killed the best friend the Free State of Louisiana had in Washington. After learning of Lincoln's death, Wells set out for the capital on May 6 to confer with the new president, Andrew Johnson. The trip was worthwhile, for Wells discovered that he and Johnson held similar views about Reconstruction. It was to be a local affair, Johnson promised, with a minimum of interference from Washington.[10]

Johnson delivered on his promise in mid-May by reorganizing the military departments of the southwest, leaving Banks without a command. Johnson took an even more important step on May 29 when he issued the first of several proclamations concerning Reconstruction that would eventually enfranchise the vast majority of former Confederate soldiers and officials, excluding only a small number who had been the leaders of the rebellion.[11]

Stripped of his authority, Banks left New Orleans and headed home to Massachusetts. Wells promptly renamed Kennedy as mayor of New Orleans and issued a proclamation that gave the rural parishes previously under Confederate control the right to reorganize their local administrations and elect officials to replace those whose terms of office had expired. Most important, Wells called for an election of state officials to be held on November 6, 1865.[12]

Between them, Wells and Johnson had restored former secessionists to the

9. *OR*, 48: pt. 2, 156, 320, 729; James A. Padgett, "Some Letters of George Stanton Denison, 1854–1866: Observations of a Yankee on Conditions in Louisiana and Texas," *Louisiana Historical Quarterly* 23 (October 1940): 1221–23; Reed, *Life of A. P. Dostie*, 181–208; *New Orleans Daily Picayune*, May 9, 10, 1865; *New Orleans Daily True Delta*, May 6, 9, 1865; Samuel M. Quincy to his mother, May 5, 1865, Quincy, Wendell, Holmes, and Upham Family Papers, LC.

10. Vandal, "New Orleans Riot," 84; Lowrey, "Political Career of James Madison Wells," 1030–32.

11. *OR*, 48: pt. 2, 475; James E. Sefton, *Andrew Johnson and the Uses of Constitutional Power* (Boston: Little, Brown, 1980), 108–9. The proclamation of May 29 dealt with the reorganization of the state government in North Carolina. Within six weeks, Johnson issued almost identical proclamations for the rest of the former Confederate States (McCrary, *Lincoln and Reconstruction*, 312–14).

12. *New Orleans Daily Picayune*, July 2, 1865; Samuel M. Quincy to his mother, June 1, 8 (postscript to letter dated June 5, 1865), Quincy, Wendell, Holmes, and Upham Family Papers; Cox, *Lincoln and Black Freedom*, 138; McCrary, *Lincoln and Reconstruction*, 315; Joe Gray Taylor, *Louisiana Reconstructed, 1863–1877* (Baton Rouge: Louisiana State University Press, 1974), 71. Wells's action followed the provisions of the 1864 constitution and thus gave evidence of his com-

positions of power they had enjoyed before the war. Wells argued in his defense that Confederate soldiers returning to their homes were "wiser and better men, frankly owing to the failure of their experiment, and all expressing a desire to atone for the errors of the past by cheerful obedience to the government." Obedient or not, most former rebels rallied in support of the new governor.[13]

Wells's drift toward the conservative end of the political spectrum and Johnson's lenient stance toward former Confederates caused the Unionists who favored a gradual reconstruction of the South to reconsider their quarrel with the Radicals. Universal male suffrage had been the major issue separating the two sides, but it had become apparent that the immediate enfranchisement of black males would be the only way the gradualists could hope to regain control of the state's political machinery. First one, then another gradualist decided to join the Radicals by announcing their support for universal male suffrage.[14]

The Radicals were pleased with the prospect of a united Unionist party and encouraged erstwhile gradualists to join them. The growing spirit of cooperation between the two groups was evident when a new political party was formed, the Friends of Universal Suffrage. Delegates to the party convention assembled on September 27, 1865, and elected Thomas J. Durant chair by acclamation. In his acceptance speech, Durant outlined his strategy for undercutting Governor Wells by appealing directly to Washington to mandate that the state enfranchise all males regardless of color. Noting that it was folly to hope that Wells would compromise on the question of enfranchising blacks, Durant argued that "the only thing left is to appeal to the decision of the United States Congress."[15]

To strengthen their hand in Washington, the delegates voted to change the name of the Friends of Universal Suffrage to the Republican Party of Louisiana. In addition, they decided to boycott the election for state officials that

mitment to that document (Brief of letter from S. Carl Schurz to Andrew Johnson, September 4, 1865, Schurz Papers; A. P. Dostie to N. P. Banks, November 26, 1865, Banks Collection).

13. *New Orleans Times,* April 20, 23, 1865; *New Orleans Tribune,* April 23, 1865; Tunnell, *Crucible of Reconstruction,* 100.

14. McCrary, *Lincoln and Reconstruction,* 321; Ripley, *Slaves and Freedmen,* 182; Simpson and Baker, "Michael Hahn," 251.

15. *Proceedings of the Convention of the Republican Party of Louisiana* (New Orleans: Tribune Office, 1865), 11, 14; *New Orleans Tribune,* September 19, 1865; Bell, *Revolution, Romanticism, and the Afro-Creole Protest Tradition,* 256; Houzeau, *My Passage,* 110–14; McCrary, *Lincoln and Reconstruction,* 321–22, 332.

Governor Wells had scheduled for November 6. As far as they were concerned, the Ordinance of Secession that Louisiana adopted in 1861 had returned the state to its previous status as a territory. The Free State of Louisiana was therefore illegal because Congress was the only body authorized by the Constitution to admit territories into the Union as states. Because Congress had not acted to readmit Louisiana, participation in the upcoming Free State election would endorse the legitimacy of an illegal administration. Instead, the delegates resolved to hold an unofficial plebiscite to select a "territorial candidate," who would go to Washington to seek recognition as the true representative of Louisiana.[16]

Henry Clay Warmoth, a former officer in the Union army and an early advocate for universal male suffrage, was nominated for the post. Both whites and blacks would be allowed to vote. Leaders of the newly organized Republican Party of Louisiana believed that black voters would gain valuable experience by participating in this, their first, election.[17]

With the Republicans holding an election of their own, the other two parties were left to their own devices. The Democratic Party in Louisiana was composed of former Confederates. The centerpiece of their campaign was compensation for former slave owners and repudiation of the constitution of 1864, which they termed "the creation of fraud, violence and corruption, and . . . not in any sense the expression of the sovereign will of the people of Louisiana." The will of the people, as the Democrats saw it, meant reasserting the supremacy of the white race. "We hold this to be a government of white people, made and to be perpetuated for the exclusive benefit of the white race," the Democratic platform read. "People of African descent cannot be considered as citizens of the United States," it declared, "and that there can, in no event, be any equality between the white and other races." The Democrats renominated Wells for governor and selected a distinguished jurist and former member of the Louisiana Supreme Court, Albert Voorhies, for the second spot on the ticket.[18]

The Democrats were opposed by the Conservative Union Party, which consisted of the remnants of the old Banks-Hahn faction that could not stom-

16. *Proceedings of the Republican Party of Louisiana*, 16–18. For controversy surrounding the decision to adopt the Republican Party name, see Bell, *Revolution, Romanticism, and the Afro-Creole Protest Tradition*, 258.

17. *Proceedings of the Republican Party of Louisiana*, 28–31; *New Orleans Tribune*, September 28, 29, 30, November 7, 1865; *New Orleans Times*, November 4, 1865.

18. Lowrey, "Political Career of James Madison Wells," 1056; *New Orleans Times*, October 4, November 6, 1865; *New Orleans Daily Southern Star*, November 6, 1866.

ach an alliance with men who endorsed black suffrage in any form, limited or universal. Anxious not to be confused with the Radicals and thus be seen as a "nigger party," the Conservative Unionists adopted a platform that was similar to the Democratic one. The only real difference between the two was that the Conservative Unionists supported for the constitution of 1864. They also nominated Wells for governor but offered James G. Talliaferro as an alternative for lieutenant governor.[19]

With two nominations, Wells won easily—22,312 votes to 5,497 for a write-in candidate, the former governor of Confederate Louisiana, Henry Watkins Allen, who had fled to Mexico. The rest of the Democratic ticket, including the new lieutenant governor, Albert Voorhies, was elected by a large majority. In the unofficial vote for territorial representative, Warmoth received a plebiscitary vote of over 19,000, only 3,000 less than Wells received in the official balloting. In addition, some 2,500 white voters wrote in Warmoth's name in the official election.[20]

Voters elected a state legislature on the same day they swept Wells into office. The new legislature was far different from the previous body. The Democrats had a clear majority, having carried every parish but one. Many of the representatives in the lower house were just back from the battlefields of the Confederacy. "The whole political power of the State, almost without exception, is in the hands of those who were in rebellion," Judge Ezra Heistand, a New Orleans Radical, protested.[21]

The newly elected legislature convened for a special session in the Mechanics' Institute on November 23, 1865. Ostensibly, its purpose was to consider issues such as the state debt, the labor question, and the election of two senators to represent Louisiana in Washington. Its main focus, however, was the attempt to reestablish control over the recently emancipated black population

19. *New Orleans Daily Picayune*, October 15, November 5, 1865; *New Orleans Times*, November 6, 1865; *New Orleans Tribune*, October 8, 1865; also see *New Orleans Daily Crescent, Daily Picayune*, and *Times*, October 17, 1865.

20. *Proceedings of the Republican Party of Louisiana*, 33–35; Taylor, *Louisiana Reconstructed*, 73; McCrary, *Lincoln and Reconstruction*, 338. Warmoth proceeded to Washington and was given the same privileges accorded representatives from the western territories, the only southern delegate to achieve recognition by the Thirty-eighth Congress (McCrary, *Lincoln and Reconstruction*, 341).

21. *HSCR*, 6, 439, 450, 466; Lowrey, "Political Career of James Madison Wells," 1064; "Rebels in Louisiana," *New Orleans Tribune*, June 4, 1865; A. P. Dostie to Banks, November 26, 1865, Banks Collection.

of the state.[22] The centerpiece of this legislation was a vagrancy law providing that "every adult freed man or woman shall furnish themselves with a comfortable home and visible means of support within 20 days after the passage of this act." Any freed man or woman who failed to do so was to be arrested, turned over to the parish, and "hired out, by public advertisement, to some citizen, being the highest bidder, for the remainder of the year."[23]

The special session of the legislature gave Wells the first indication that he could not control the former Confederates whom he had befriended. Announcing that the vagrancy act conflicted with federal regulations regarding freedmen, Wells refused to sign the measure. He also vetoed a bill to suspend the collection of taxes for the years 1861 through 1864 because he believed that it favored former rebels.[24]

When the regular session convened in January 1866, the break between the governor and the legislature was complete. At first they disagreed over minor matters, but things came to a head in February, when the legislature passed a bill calling for municipal elections in New Orleans. This measure was designed to oust Kennedy and the rest of Wells's appointees. Wells vetoed the bill, but the legislature passed it unanimously over his veto.[25]

Stung by the defeat, Wells began to reconsider his options. Until now, he had opposed universal male suffrage because he had assumed that the recently freed slaves would support their former masters. But the rapidity with which secessionists had recaptured control of the state's political machinery made Wells realize that black suffrage was his only hope for a promising political future.[26]

22. *New Orleans Tribune*, December 5, 1865. For Michael Hahn's sarcastic account of the legislature's efforts and a response to his accusations, see "Ex-Governor Hahn on Louisiana Legislature's Relating to Freedmen," *New Orleans Tribune*, May 2, 1866, and "The Negro in Louisiana," *New Orleans Daily Crescent*, June 8, 1866, respectively.

23. *Journal of the House of Representatives of the State of Louisiana, Extra Session, November 23, 1865* (New Orleans: J. O. Nixon, 1865), 3, 73; *Acts Passed by the General Assembly of the State of Louisiana, Extra Session, 1865* (New Orleans: J. O. Nixon, 1866), 18. Even more stringent, discriminatory laws were passed by local governments, particularly in the rural parishes (McCrary, *Lincoln and Reconstruction*, 326–27).

24. Tunnell, *Crucible of Reconstruction*, 100–101; Vandal, "New Orleans Riot," 127–29; *New Orleans Daily Crescent*, December 25, 1865.

25. Taylor, *Louisiana Reconstructed*, 81; Tunnell, *Crucible of Reconstruction*, 103; Vandal, "New Orleans Riot," 137–39.

26. *New Orleans Daily Picayune*, July 12, 1865; Taylor, *Louisiana Reconstructed*, 103–4. See "Louisiana Radicals Losing Caste," *New Orleans Times*, April 24, 1866, for discussion of how the municipal elections in March had demoralized the Radicals.

Once again, free blacks in New Orleans led the way. Although some free blacks believed that limited suffrage based on strict qualifications was still the best way to gain political equality with whites, the majority of free blacks in New Orleans determined to join forces with the freedmen and present a united black front. The result was the formation of the National Equal Rights League, which expected the United States Congress to guarantee black suffrage without restrictions of property ownership or education. Who "would be selfish enough to vote when thousands of his brethren cannot?" the *Tribune* asked rhetorically. "Who is willing to abandon his race for a short and void gratification?" The most effective course of action, according to the *Tribune*, was to maintain racial unity and petition the United States Congress for universal male suffrage.[27]

Reluctantly, Wells agreed. It was better to try to win the black vote than to surrender control of the state to men who had only a few months earlier been fighting to destroy the Union. "By the Eternal, he [Wells] intended to beat the Rebels and keep them from power," Warmoth confided to his diary, "if in so doing he destroyed the state government and produced anarchy for twenty years."[28]

Like others before him, Wells had come reluctantly to this opinion. But once arrived at, there was no going back. "There is no middle course," Wells argued. "Anything short of universal suffrage will, in my opinion, fail to effect any satisfactory political results." His conversion did not go unnoticed, for the *Baton Rouge Weekly Advocate* reported in late June that Wells had "sold himself out to the Cutler-Hahn nigger suffrage party."[29]

Deciding that blacks should be given the right to vote and actually making it happen were two very different issues. But with the governor now on their side, proponents of black suffrage hit on a plan. Their idea was to reconvene the constitutional convention of 1864 and amend the document in such a way as to disfranchise former rebels and give black males the vote.[30]

The scheme was based on a technicality. When the constitutional convention adjourned in July 1864, it did not do so sine dire. Rather, it adjourned

27. *New Orleans Tribune*, January 15, February 19, 21, 1865; Ripley, *Slaves and Freedmen*, 178–80.

28. Taylor, *Louisiana Reconstructed*, 104; diary entry for March 28, 1866, Henry Clay Warmoth Papers, SHC.

29. *HSCR*, 439; Lowrey, "Political Career of James Madison Wells," 1076; "Gathering of the Buzzards," *Baton Rouge Weekly Advocate*, June 30, 1866.

30. *Nation* 3 (August 16, 1866): 121; *New Orleans Daily Picayune*, July 7 (afternoon edition), 10, 1866.

with the understanding that "it should be at the call of the president, whose duty it shall be to reconvene the convention for any cause, or in case the constitution shall not be ratified, or for the purpose of taking such measures as may be necessary for the formation of a Civil government for the State of Louisiana." Supporters of universal male suffrage saw reconvening the constitutional convention as their only hope of enfranchising blacks and disfranchising former secessionists.[31]

Most whites in New Orleans believed that reconvening the convention was equivalent to organizing a coup d'état. "With the termination of the war, and the withdrawal of martial law, the military authority over civil affairs, which grew out of a state of war, ceased," an editorial in the *Daily Picayune* argued. "When the authority of Gen. Banks over the subject ceased," it continued, "the powers which he had vested in others ceased of course. The convention which was created by military order No. 35 had therefore a double sentence of extinction. It had executed the work for which it was created, and was necessarily dissolved thereby; and the authority by which its existence was supported has disappeared."[32]

Ironically, Thomas J. Durant agreed with the conservatives. "We must not indulge in expressions which would induce the public to believe that we have abandoned our former opinions," he argued. "Moreover, a convention, although legitimate in the beginning, is no longer in existence after its work has been accomplished. It cannot perpetuate itself." If some Radicals sanctioned the scheme to reconvene the body, Durant observed, they did so as individuals.[33]

Even the convention's president, Edmund Durell, was uncertain about the legality of the proposal. When a group favoring reconvening the convention approached Durell in June and asked for his support, he answered, "No sir." Durell did not think that it could be brought off without a riot. "It will be as much as your life is worth to be there," he told the group.[34]

Rebuffed by both Durant and Durell, the supporters of black suffrage

31. As noted in the previous chapter, the new constitution had been ratified on September 5, 1864, by a vote of 6,836 in favor to 1,566 opposed (Vandal, "New Orleans Riot," 54); see also Rable, *But There Was No Peace*, 46–47.

32. *HSCR*, 255; *New Orleans Daily Picayune*, July 29, 1866.

33. Vandal, "New Orleans Riot," 148. Durant believed that ratification of the document in September 1864 was a hoax because of widespread election irregularities (*New Orleans Tribune*, April 14, 1865).

34. *HSCR*, 149, 262. Durell telegraphed several of the leading Radicals in Congress in June to ask for their views but received no reply (Vandal, "New Orleans Riot," 162).

called a preliminary meeting to elect a president pro tem and to decide on their next step. Thirty-nine delegates to the convention met at the Mechanics' Institute on June 26, 1866. Judge Durell's refusal to participate presented a problem, for the resolution giving them the authority to reconvene specified that it could do so only at the call of the president. Furthermore, those who attended the meeting constituted less than half of the ninety-five elected members. Undeterred, the delegates elected Rufus K. Howell, associate justice on the state supreme court and an original member of the convention, as the new president.[35]

Judge Howell's election was controversial for two reasons. For one, Howell had taken an oath of allegiance to the Confederacy after Louisiana seceded so he could keep his seat as a district judge. Furthermore, Howell had resigned from the convention in May 1864, citing the obligations of his official duties. The delegates accepted his resignation but changed their minds a few days later when Howell changed his. Even then, his reinstatement was out of order, given the rules under which the body had been organized.[36]

Undaunted by the question of whether they had any standing legally, the delegates who assembled on June 26 directed Judge Howell to issue a proclamation calling for the convention to reconvene at twelve noon on July 30, 1866, in the Mechanics' Institute. They also called on Governor Wells to authorize the election of additional delegates from parishes that were under Confederate control in 1864 and thus had not been represented in the original body. Howell drafted the document as directed and issued the proclamation two weeks later on July 7.[37]

Howell and the thirty-eight members of the convention who met on June 26 were on shaky ground. Nevertheless, they pressed ahead because they had something else in their favor—the support, they thought, of the United States Congress. Many of the Radicals in Congress agreed with the Friends of Universal Suffrage. Louisiana had ceased to be a state when she seceded and had thereby reverted to the status of a territory. As a territory, Louisiana came under the direct authority of Congress. The delegates who favored black suffrage hoped that Congress would intervene to approve the amended constitu-

35. *HSCR*, 11, 46, 60; Vandal, "New Orleans Riot," 162. Howell was not a native of New Orleans, having arrived in the city in 1850 (Conrad, *Dictionary of Louisiana Biography*, 1:412).
36. *HSCR*, 388. Absenteeism became a major problem as the convention proceeded with its business. On April 29, 1864, the delegates passed a motion that docked members' per diem for all days on which they failed to answer the roll. Howell resigned a week later but was reinstated on May 9, 1864 (*DCCL*, 117, 191, 204).
37. *HSCR*, 46–47, 53–55.

tion, bypassing the need to have it ratified by a vote of the people, which they knew would never happen.[38]

Not everyone was willing to ignore the question of the convention's legality. Judge Edmund Abell, the outspoken member of the convention, staunchly opposed black suffrage. "The admission to that high privilege to millions of negroes who are not only ignorant but many of them stupid," he had declared in January 1866, "would be a drawback to civilization, a reproach and disgrace to republican government." Believing that blacks were incapable of knowing what was best for themselves, Abell argued that "they would be dupes of arch and wily politicians, or the dangerous instruments of power for wealthy, violent or roguish demagogues."[39]

Abell was in the position to follow up his rhetoric with action. The conservative lawyer had run for a seat in the Free State legislature in February 1864, but Michael Hahn had intervened to prevent his election. Abell had threatened to contest the outcome but dropped the case when Hahn promised a judgeship in the First District. Coincidentally, the Mechanics' Institute was located in the First District. Thus, by a twist of fate, the body that had rejected Abell's conservative agenda in 1864 now found itself scheduled to reconvene in Abell's judicial district.[40]

Abell was determined to stop the convention from reconvening. To that end, he issued an order on July 2 for 150 jurors to appear the next day. The names were drawn from a large tin wheel containing slips of paper with the names of registered voters in the parish. Sixteen names were selected from this panel to serve on a grand jury that was to try cases for one month.[41]

Abell began his charge to the grand jury on July 3 by noting some of the routine responsibilities of the duty, such as visiting prisons within the parish and reporting on the treatment of prisoners. Then he brought up the subject of the constitutional convention.

38. *HSCR*, 151, 409, 515; "Loyal Letter No. 15: The Convention," *New Orleans Tribune*, July 23, 1864; "The Call for a Convention of Southern Radicals," *New Orleans Bee*, July 17, 1866. Questions regarding the constitutional status of the seceded states were considerably more complex than this brief explanation suggests. An analysis and discussion of the issues can be found in Belz, *Reconstructing the Union*.

39. Abell's charge to the grand jury on January 9, 1866, published in the *New Orleans Daily Crescent*, January 10, 1866; also in the *New Orleans Daily Southern Star* and *Daily Picayune*, January 10, 1866.

40. *New Orleans Daily True Delta*, April 2, 1865; Vandal, "New Orleans Riot," 56.

41. *MCR*, 59–61.

I further charge you that the constitution [of the state of Louisiana] makes no provision for the continuance of the convention of 1864 . . . and that any effort upon the part of that defunct body to assemble, for the purpose of altering or amending the constitution, is subversive of good order and dangerous to the peace of the State, and that any overt act tending to subvert the constitution by any officers of the State who have sworn to support it renders them liable to the criminal laws of the State for misdemeanor in office and perjury.[42]

The members of the grand jury listened attentively to the charge. Judge Abell was saying what they wanted to hear, for these jurors were hostile to the convention. As the military commission that investigated the riot was to discover, the master list of registered voters from which the slate of jurors was selected had not been purged of persons who were ineligible to serve as a result of their support of the Confederacy during the war. Consequently, the jury was packed with former Confederates. Three and possibly six of the sixteen jurors had served in the Confederate Army of Tennessee; four others had served in the Louisiana militia. The foreman, Francis Rawle, had been a captain in the Army of Northern Virginia.[43]

There was another problem with the grand jury in addition to its composition. The court's term ended the day after Abell gave his charge, July 4, and by law, the grand jury could not hear cases while the court was not in session. As a result, there developed a curious situation in which an illegal grand jury attempted to issue writs against members of an equally illegal constitutional convention.[44]

Judge Abell pressed ahead nevertheless. On July 23, a week before the con-

---

42. *HSCR*, 275.

43. *MCR*, 65–66. Members of the grand jury identified as definitely having served in the Confederate army were Francis Rawle, the foreman (captain, 1st Louisiana Infantry [Nelligan's] and Righton's Louisiana Infantry [3:253]), L. E. Charbonet (22d and 23d Louisiana Infantry [1:325]), and Anthony Prados, Jr. (22d and 23d Louisiana Infantry [3:192]). Those with possible service were Charles W. Hopkins (5th Louisiana Infantry [2:351]), Isaac N. Phillips (6th Louisiana Infantry [3:134]), and Philip Power, Jr. (Pointe Coupee Light Artillery [3:188]). John R. Conway, H. E. Flores, J. G. Vienne, and J. Viosca probably served in the Louisiana militia. Members of the grand jury with no record of prior service included Henry Aubert, Victor David, Victor J. Forstall, S. B. Frost, Charles Rouyer, and B. P. Voorhies. (Volume and page numbers in brackets refer to Andrew B. Booth, *Records of Louisiana Confederate Soldiers and Louisiana Confederate Commands*, 3 vols. [1920; rpr., Spartanburg, S.C.: Reprint Co., 1984]).

44. *MCR*, 59; Tunnell, *Crucible of Reconstruction*, 103–4; Gilles Vandal, "The Origins of the New Orleans Riot of 1866, Revisited," *Louisiana History* 22 (Spring 1981): 140.

vention was to reconvene, he reassembled the grand jury to provide more "specific instructions relative to your powers to suppress unlawful assemblies dangerous to the peace and good order of the State." In short, Judge Abell attacked the legality of reconvening the convention. "Any attempt to alter the constitution of the State in defiance of its provisions, by any body of men unauthorized by the provisions of the constitution, or powers emanating directly from the people through the ballot-box, is illegal and unconstitutional, and punishable by law." Abell went on to assure the members of the grand jury that the military would not interfere with them should they choose to indict delegates who choose to reconvene. In closing, Abell reminded the jurors that he was a member of the convention of 1864. "With feelings of kindness towards each and every member, I earnestly hope that they will desist from their illegal purposes and that you may not be required to enforce any law of the State in vindication of its peace and dignity. But if meet they must, apply the law justly and firmly; the constitution must be vindicated."[45]

Despite his confident charge to the grand jury, Abell was in a bit of a legal fix himself. Earlier in the month, R. F. Daunoy, a staunch Unionist and formerly the coroner for Orleans Parish, had signed an affidavit in the U.S. Fifth Circuit Court charging Abell with having violated the Civil Rights Act of 1866.[46] Believing that Abell's charge to the grand jury on July 3 "was conceived by a wicked, malicious, and politically prejudicial mind and heart," Daunoy argued that Abell's language was "revolutionary in its character, tends to a breach of the peace, inciting and sensational seditious, and gives aid and comfort to the enemies of the United States, and is in open violation of the constitution and laws of the United States, and of this State, and is treasonable." The U.S. commissioner ordered Abell arrested and brought before the federal court on July 20. The judge posted a $500 bond and was released until his case came before the federal grand jury.[47]

The specter of the intervention of federal courts in the local affairs of Louisiana loomed large in the minds of many whites during the spring and summer of 1866, increasing tensions and aggravating concerns related to the constitu-

45. *HSCR*, 275–77.

46. Daunoy was raised in Paris but had lived in New Orleans since 1847. Although forced to serve in the Louisiana militia, he had taken an oath of allegiance almost as soon as Butler arrived in the city (*HSCR*, 135–37).

47. "The Judiciary: United States Circuit Court," *New Orleans Daily Picayune*, December 14, 1866. The federal grand jury heard Abell's case in December 1866, five months after the riot, and concluded that there were no grounds for finding a true bill (*New Orleans Daily Picayune*, December 14, 1866).

tional convention. Abell's case was only one of several giving the impression that the people who supported black suffrage could resort to the Civil Rights Act to thwart state laws and to protect themselves from prosecution.[48]

Many whites in New Orleans were furious at the prospect. "[Abell's] arrest is a gross outrage," the *New Orleans Times* reported on July 21, 1866. "It is undoubtedly a scheme of the plotters and disorganizers now at work in this City, and who, for self aggrandizement, stop at no measure, it matters not how lawless, that will advance their schemes. That such reckless and lawless acts must recoil upon their own heads," the *Times* warned, "seems to us inevitable."[49]

48. Rable, *But There Was No Peace*, 10; Vandal, "Origins of the New Orleans Riot," 154; *New Orleans Daily Picayune*, July 3, 8, 1866; *New Orleans Times*, July 3, 8, 1866.

49. "A High Handed Proceeding: Arrest of Judge Abell," *New Orleans Times*, July 21, 1866.

4

We Are in Revolutionary Times

W ILLIAM MITHOFF picked up his son from school on Friday afternoon, July 27, 1866. The question his son asked when he got into the carriage disturbed Mithoff.

Mithoff was born in Germany and had come to America as a young man to make his fortune. He had enjoyed modest success as a small farmer in Jefferson Parish outside the city, enabling him to send his youngest son to school in New Orleans.[1]

Mithoff was a strong Union man from the beginning; he had always opposed secession. That made his life a bit rough, particularly in the early days of the war. The fall of New Orleans in 1862, however, changed everything. When federal troops occupied his parish, Mithoff's Unionism became a virtue. A supporter of Michael Hahn, Mithoff had been elected to the Free State legislature in 1864, serving in both sessions. But things changed dramatically once the war was over. When Mithoff ran for Congress in the fall of 1865, his Unionism was again a liability.

Mithoff campaigned hard for a seat in Congress, traveling through his district behind a protective screen of Union soldiers. He tried to sell his vision of

1. *HSCR*, 370–72.

a new state, one that would be brought back into the Union quickly with benefits and freedoms for all. But Mithoff encountered a hardened attitude among the men who had just returned from service in the Confederate army. They were determined to fight the federal government in Washington and swore not to support anyone who had remained loyal to the Union during the war. To them, Mithoff was a traitor, and now they saw to it that he lost.

Mithoff was disappointed to lose the election, but he was even more concerned over the growing hatred of blacks he observed among whites in his district. The paternalism among planters that existed before the war was gone, along with the protection against random violence it had provided. Mithoff had seen the increase of violence firsthand. "The negroes in my parish had a church," he reported, "and when I went down there a month or more ago, I saw the church had disappeared. I asked what had become of the church. They said they had burned it down. They said that they would not allow any nigger churches there." Experiences such as that gave Mithoff reason to be worried about the question his son asked as they were driving home. "Why, Daddy, are they going to kill all the Union men and negroes in the city on Monday?" The children were talking about it in school, his son told him. Mithoff decided then and there that he was not going into New Orleans on Monday.[2]

As Mithoff and his son hurried home, Governor Madison Wells returned to New Orleans from an extended trip he had taken to Alexandria to look after his plantation in Rapides Parish. He immediately went to his office in the Mechanics' Institute.[3]

A considerable amount of work had piled up on the governor's desk, but before tackling it Wells found time to issue writs for an election on September 3, 1866, to replace members of the constitutional convention who had died or resigned. In addition, the governor authorized the election of delegates from parishes that had been under Confederate control when the original body had been elected.[4]

The stage was set. Initially, most white Louisianians had thought that reconvening the convention was an absurdity.[5] But what had seemed at first to

2. *HSCR*, 372.
3. *HSCR*, 438; "Confusion of the Convention Plotters," *New Orleans Daily Picayune*, July 7, 1866.
4. "Unfolding of the Plot," *New Orleans Daily Picayune*, July 28, 1866; *HSCR*, 274. The original convention was to have consisted of 150 delegates, but only 95 were elected because of Confederate control of the state in 1864 (*HSCR*, 60).
5. *HSCR*, 387.

be a futile, albeit disturbing, attempt to reverse the gains recent rebels had made in securing the reins of government now had the sanction of the governor. The stakes increased dramatically with Wells's call for elections.

While Wells shuffled the papers on his desk in New Orleans, President Andrew Johnson sat in his office in the White House almost two thousand miles away, talking with an emissary from Louisiana.

Joseph Adolphus Rozier was a lawyer from New Orleans with connections to both Unionists and former Confederates. He had been elected as a member of Louisiana's secession convention in 1861 but had urged compromise instead of secession. Although the other delegates ignored his advice, Rozier continued to express his opposition to secession and voted against the ordinance.[6]

Nevertheless, Rozier still had many friends in New Orleans, and when Benjamin F. Butler occupied the city in 1862, Rozier tried to get him to ease some of the restrictions Butler had imposed on Confederate sympathizers. Rozier was also active in the local Union Association but had resigned when the association called for the gradual emancipation of slaves. Because of his conservative bent, Rozier's Unionism was forgiven when former Confederates captured the legislature in 1865. It was useful to have someone with his connections in Washington to plead their case before the president.[7]

Rozier had with him a letter from the lieutenant governor of Louisiana, Albert Voorhies, in which Voorhies explained that a small group of former members of the 1864 constitutional convention had determined to reconvene that body for the purpose of enfranchising blacks and disfranchising former Confederates. "In ordinary times such a proceeding as this, more of a small fraction of a body, which itself did not at any time represent a serious constituency, should be considered as a solemn farce," Voorhies wrote. "But, at the present day, when it is considered that the National government is on the brink of a revolution whose object is to pervert the organic law," he asserted, "and when it is apparent, nay even proclaimed, that the revolution to be inaugurated here forms part of a programme of the Radical revolutionists at Wash-

6. *HSCR*, 221; Ralph A. Wooster, *The Secession Conventions of the South* (Princeton, N.J.: Princeton University Press, 1962), 109–10.

7. McCrary, *Lincoln and Reconstruction*, 99, 174; *Minutes of General Committee of Union Associations*, July 24, 1863, NYHS; Rozier to Butler, June 9, 1862, Special Order No. 96, June 12, 1862, Butler to Stanton, June 10, 1862, Butler to Rozier and Durant, June 3, 1862, all in Benjamin Franklin Butler, *Private and Official Correspondence of Gen. Benjamin F. Butler During a Period of the Civil War*, ed. Jessie Ames Marshall, 5 vols. (Norwood, Mass.: Plimpton Press, 1917), 1:565–74.

ington;—it becomes a question of prudence not to treat this matter too lightly, but, taking things at the worst, to prepare for all possible emergencies."[8]

Rozier showed Voorhies's letter to the president and then interjected an opinion of his own. The convention "had no shadow of right of meeting together," Rozier stated flatly. "It was all humbuggery from beginning to end, a mere sham." Would the duly elected government of Louisiana be allowed to put down the conspiracy, he asked the president, or would the U.S. Army stationed in New Orleans interfere? As commander in chief, Johnson could settle the matter once and for all.[9]

A staunch Unionist who called secession treason, Johnson nevertheless believed that the federal government was too strong. Johnson had opposed secession, it was true, but not because he lacked a devotion to the principle of states' rights. Johnson had opposed secession because he hated the planter class, which was why his amnesty proclamation in May had excluded fourteen classes of former rebels, most notably major Confederate officials and owners of taxable property valued at more than $20,000. In reality, Johnson had reenfranchised the white yeomen, men of humble origins like himself, and disfranchised the old planter elite.[10]

Johnson's dislike of the planter class did not mean that he was opposed to slavery. During his successful campaign for a seat in the Senate in 1857, Johnson had called slavery a natural element of society throughout history, brought about because of the inferiority of the black race. In fact, the president had owned five slaves himself before the war. Although he had accepted the reality of emancipation, Andrew Johnson had not been and would never be a friend of the black man.[11]

Not surprisingly, Johnson did not believe that blacks should have the right to vote. "The query comes up whether these two races," Johnson had stated in an interview the previous February, "without preparation, without time for passion and excitement to disappear, and without time for the slightest improvement, whether the one should be turned loose upon the other and be thrown together at the ballot box with this enmity and hate existing between them." The president was convinced that enfranchising black males would

8. Albert Voorhies to J. A. Rozier, July 13, 1866, Andrew Johnson Presidential Collection, LC.

9. *HSCR*, 221, 225.

10. Foner, *Reconstruction*, 181–83; McCrary, *Lincoln and Reconstruction*, 305–6.

11. Lawanda Cox and John H. Cox, *Politics, Principle, and Prejudice, 1865–1866: Dilemma of Reconstruction America* (New York: Free Press of Glencoe, 1963), 152–53; Sefton, *Andrew Johnson*, 48–49, 63, 118.

create a war between the races. Black suffrage, he reasoned, should not be forced on whites without their consent. "I might go down to the ballot box to-morrow and vote directly for universal suffrage," he declared. "But if a great majority of this people said no, I should consider it would be tyrannical and arbitrary in me to attempt to force it upon them without their will. It is a fundamental point in my creed that the will of the people must be obeyed when fairly expressed. Is there anything wrong or unfair in that?"[12]

Most white people in Louisiana certainly did not see anything wrong or unfair about Johnson's policy on Reconstruction. Former Confederates praised the president for his noninterference with their efforts to regain political control of the state. Many Louisiana Unionists also endorsed his policy, for they believed that federal interference in local affairs would make the process of bringing the state back into the Union more difficult. The only ones who did not like the hands-off approach were black men and women, for Johnson's policy meant that local authorities could deal with them as they pleased.[13]

Johnson knew what was happening in New Orleans. The previous December, Thomas W. Conway, who recently had been in charge of the Freedmen's Bureau in Louisiana and was a staunch supporter of black suffrage, had met with the president to apprise him of the situation. Conway had told Johnson that there were secret societies in the Crescent City bent on subverting the federal government. He had explained that the feeling of whites in general was extremely hostile to Washington and that they would make every attempt to undercut Johnson's efforts to make them loyal citizens of the Union.[14]

Johnson had told Conway that he knew of these societies, but he did not believe that they were organized for any bad purpose. Rather they were benevolent organizations interested in caring for the widows and orphans of Con-

12. "President Johnson and Negro Suffrage," *New Orleans Daily Southern Star*, February 15, 1866. For a discussion of Johnson's position regarding black suffrage, see Cox and Cox, *Politics, Principle, and Prejudice*, 154–63.

13. *HSCR*, 224, 284; Foner, *Reconstruction*, 184. For the evolution of Johnson's policy of reconciliation with the South, see David Donald, *The Politics of Reconstruction, 1863–1867* (Baton Rouge: Louisiana State University Press, 1965), 17–25.

14. *HSCR*, 525–28. Conway was a thirty-year-old chaplain in the Union army who had been instrumental in setting up the first schools for blacks in Louisiana. Initially, he had cooperated with Banks as director of Banks's labor system but joined the Radicals over the issue of black suffrage. Conway was appointed the first state commissioner of the Freedmen's Bureau in March 1865 but in October was removed from office because of his persistent advocacy of black civil rights as well as numerous fiscal improprieties (McCrary, *Lincoln and Reconstruction*, 156–57, 322–23, 330–31, 336–37; Howard A. White, *The Freedmen's Bureau in Louisiana* [Baton Rouge: Louisiana State University Press, 1970], 8, 21).

federate veterans. The war had settled the question of loyalty, Johnson had told Conway. Most white citizens of Louisiana had taken the oath of allegiance, and it was in their best interest to behave themselves. Consequently, the new state government could take care of itself. Furthermore, Johnson believed that he did not have the right as president to interfere in local affairs.[15]

Conway had disagreed. He had warned that Johnson's policy was sustaining the rebellion. Former secessionists were under the misapprehension that the president sided with them; they even honored Andrew Johnson and Jefferson Davis together in the same drinking toasts. It was Johnson's turn to disagree. His policy was "doing very well," he had told Conway. Order was being maintained, persons were taking the oath of allegiance, and soon the reconstructed government of Louisiana would be in a position to gain readmission to the Union.[16]

It had been six months since his conversation with Conway, and the president had not changed his mind. The federal government must recognize the authority of local courts in New Orleans to regulate matters that were internal to the state of Louisiana. The local authorities should and must be supported. The military would not interfere, Johnson assured Rozier.[17]

Rozier hurried from his meeting with the president and went to the telegraph office. He wanted to get word to Voorhies that Johnson was behind them; the president would order the army to stand clear.[18]

Supporters of the constitutional convention assembled at the Mechanics' Institute Friday night for a rally. The institute was an imposing structure. Constructed in 1857 by the famous New Orleans architect James Gallier, Jr., it stood on the river side of Dryades Street (now University Place) midway between Canal and Common. The building consisted of three floors, although it was actually four stories high. The main hall, where the Louisiana House of Representatives met, was a large room two stories high that ran almost the entire length of the building. Beneath the main hall on the ground floor were a series of smaller rooms used for committee meetings. The Louisiana Senate met in one of these rooms, and Governor Wells's office was located on this floor toward the rear of the building.[19]

15. *HSCR*, 528.
16. *Ibid.*
17. *HSCR*, 225.
18. *New Orleans Times*, July 30, 1866.
19. Construction of the Mechanics' Institute began in 1856 and ended in 1858 ("The Architecture of James Gallier, Jr.," *Gallier House* 4 [Fall 1983]: 1). Originally, the building was used by the New Orleans Mechanics Society, an educational and charitable association consisting of

The rally consisted of two meetings that went on simultaneously. The one in the main hall was more of a briefing than a rally. Its purpose was to inform the audience about plans to reconvene the convention and to adopt a set of resolutions in support of the venture. Free State governor Michael Hahn was there, as were other supporters of the convention—Colonel A. P. Field and R. King Cutler. The audience was composed mostly of professionals and small businessmen. The speakers endorsed black suffrage but urged restraint. Be patient, keep calm, one of them told the black members of the audience. Do not force the issue too strongly, for doing so might jeopardize their success.[20]

Colonel A. P. Field's speech was typical. "You are gaining friends every day," he told the gathering. There is no need for violence, he assured them. "Although there is but a few thousand devoted to your cause today," he proclaimed, "there will be a great many more within a short time." The audience cheered. In retrospect, Field considered his speech to be "very mild," given the mood of the time.[21]

R. King Cutler, a member of the convention and an unsuccessful claimant for a seat in the U.S. Senate, spoke last. Cutler stated that the time had come to amend the state's constitution to enfranchise black men. In addition, he proposed that the state adopt the Fourteenth Amendment because it would prevent former rebels who had been officeholders before the war from regaining their old positions. It would be a good idea to disfranchise former Confederates in general, he added. Finally, Cutler blamed President Johnson's lenient policy for the reversals Louisiana loyalists had suffered at the polls since the end of the war. Cutler ended his address by reminding the audience that their cause was righteous and that the convention was legal.[22]

The meeting ended with the adoption of seven resolutions. "*Resolved*," the first began, "that the seventy-thousand citizens of Louisiana, qualified to vote,

---

"Mechanics, manufacturers and artists of the city and suburbs of New Orleans." It was converted to public use in 1862 (*New Orleans Daily Delta*, September 25, 1862), and by 1866 the main hall was being used for charity balls and other public events in addition to its function as a meeting place for the House of Representatives (e.g., see *New Orleans Daily Crescent*, May 17, 1866). The state government moved from its quarters in City Hall to the Mechanics' Institute in late March 1866 (*New Orleans Daily Crescent*, March 28, 1866; *New Orleans Daily Picayune*, March 29, 1866). For descriptions of the Mechanics' Institute, see *MCR*, 149, and *HSCR*, 493. A rough sketch of the floor plan can be found in the Sandborn Insurance Maps for New Orleans.

20. *HSCR*, 15–16, 23, 39, 44, 476; Vandal, "Origins of the New Orleans Riot," 148–49.

21. *HSCR*, 407; *MCR*, 280. A. P. Field was a prosperous lawyer and conservative Unionist who followed Hahn's lead by joining the Radicals when it became apparent that former sessionists had regained control of the state's political machinery (McCrary, *Lincoln and Reconstruction*, 175, 178–79; Taylor, *Louisiana Reconstructed*, 22, 53–56).

22. *HSCR*, 32; Taylor, *Louisiana Reconstructed*, 125.

but disfranchised on account of color, twenty-thousand of whom risked their lives in her behalf in the war against the rebellion deserve as a debt of gratitude, that participation in the Government which citizenship confers." And so each resolution went, endorsing the plan to reconvene the convention, expressing gratitude to Governor Wells and Judge Howell, and thanking the United States Congress for protecting the civil rights of "loyal men" and establishing the Freedmen's Bureau. The seventh and final resolution stated explicitly what the preceding six had only implied. "*Resolved*, That, until the doctrine of the political equality of all citizens, irrespective of color, is recognized in this State by the establishment therein of universal suffrage, there will and can be no permanent peace."[23]

The meeting outside the Mechanics' Institute was very different than the one inside. A crowd of three to five hundred men, black and white, had gathered in front of a wooden stage erected especially for the occasion. Coal-oil lamps were placed on the stage to illuminate the speakers. Boys with torches stood on the pavement to provide more light.[24]

The temper of the speeches outside was more militant than of those inside. They started with an address by Judge Ezra Heistand in which he explained the validity of the argument for black suffrage. Heistand was followed by Cutler's law partner, John Henderson.[25]

Henderson was a strong Union man whose outspoken views during the war had caused him to be labeled insane. As a result, he had spent almost the entire war in an asylum in Mississippi. Although Henderson was clearly out of step with the prevailing mores of his region, he was not crazy. He realized that a national policy without local support was doomed. "We may have Union Congressmen as already suggested," Henderson had written Nathaniel P. Banks in November 1865, "but Sir, we should have a *Union* local government over our people. To have Union men at Washington in the National Counsels and rebels to govern us at home would not and should not be tolerated by a loyal President & Congress of these United States."[26]

Gaining Unionist rule at home was proving difficult, however, and Henderson had been one of the most ardent advocates for amending the Constitution to enfranchise blacks and to disfranchise rebels. In reference to reconven-

23. "The Radical Mob," *New Orleans Times*, July 28, 1866.

24. *MCR*, 194; *HSCR*, 482.

25. *New Orleans Daily Crescent*, July 28, 1866. Judge Heistand is incorrectly identified as "Judge Hawkins" (*HSCR*, 1).

26. *HSCR*, 389; Henderson to Banks, November 26, 1865, Banks Collection.

ing the convention, Henderson had recently told one acquaintance that "it was a revolutionary movement, but we are in revolutionary times."[27]

The night was warm, eighty-six degrees, and Henderson warmed to his task. He denounced the prevailing rebel sentiment in the city and urged an end to the political domination of former Confederates. He had been opposed to black suffrage during the convention, Henderson reminded the audience, and he had been opposed to disfranchisement of the rebels as well. But his experience with "rebel ingratitude" since the end of the war had changed his mind. "I would rather have a good loyal black man to represent me in Washington," Henderson declared, "than a disloyal white man."[28]

F. W. Tilton, exemplary of the disloyal white man Henderson referred to, listened with muted rage from the balcony of his house on the corner of Dryades and Canal, half a block from the platform in front of the institute from which Henderson was speaking. Tilton later swore that at one point Henderson announced that "every man, woman, and child in the city of New Orleans were rebels, traitors, scoundrels, and ought to be sent to hell."[29]

Dr. A. P. Dostie was next. Born in New York of French-German descent, Dostie had moved to New Orleans in 1852 but was forced to flee the city in 1861 because of his vigorous opposition to secession. Dostie had returned to New Orleans after it was occupied by Union troops and quickly became a strong supporter of Nathaniel P. Banks. Dostie had worked hard in September 1864 to make sure that the constitution was ratified, and now the forty-five-year-old dentist endorsed reconvening the convention to complete the work it had failed to finish two years earlier.[30]

Dostie was an intense speaker. Handsome, of medium height, straight as an arrow, he had dark, piercing eyes that seemed to flash with the excitement of his oration. He was not prone to equivocate. "If you are right," Dostie was fond of saying, "you cannot be too radical."[31]

Tonight there was no question in Dostie's mind that he was right. "We

---

27. *HSCR*, 299.

28. "The Universal Suffrage Meeting," *New Orleans Daily Crescent*, July 28, 1866. Temperature from the *New Orleans Bee*, July 28, 1866.

29. *MCR*, 194–95; *HSCR*, 1. The platform had been erected earlier that evening especially for the occasion (*HSCR*, 312–13).

30. Harrington, *Fighting Politician*, 101, 149; Reed, *Life of A. P. Dostie*, 13, 17, 20. Dostie announced the resumption of his dentistry practice in November 1863 (*New Orleans Times*, November 2, 1863). For Dostie's close relationship with Banks, see Banks to the Editors of the *Republican*, August 1, 1866, Banks Collection.

31. Reed, *Life of A. P. Dostie*, 320; also see *Address of Dr. A[nthony] P. Dostie delivered before the Republican Association of New Orleans, May 9, 1866* (New Orleans[?]: N.p., 1866[?]).

have got you your freedom; we have fought for your freedom," Dostie shouted, "now will you fight for your votes?" "We will; we will," came the response from the crowd, followed by a chant "Fight to vote! Fight to vote!," again and again. Dostie then invited the crowd to come to the institute on Monday to show their support for the convention. It was like an old-time political rally with cheers and shouts. This time, however, the cries were from black men who had been excluded from the political process and who now saw the prospect of suffrage within their grasp.[32]

By ten-thirty the speeches were over, and a group of two or three hundred mostly black men started off on a torchlight procession from the institute, down Canal and along St. Charles to City Hall. Dostie led the way with a United States flag by his side. The mood in the procession was defiant. As the marchers passed whites standing on the banquette, they cheered and jeered, waved their hats, and gestured.[33]

Arriving at City Hall, Dostie climbed the steps and gave an impromptu speech. The address was not long, but it was passionate. Referring to the black marchers as his brothers, Dostie exhorted them to stand firm in the face of opposition to their cause. "Now friends, go home peaceably, quietly; make no noise; disturb no person; but . . . I learn . . . that there are prowling bands of armed men out to waylay you," Dostie warned. "If you are insulted by any of these bands of men, pay no attention to them," he advised. "Go home right by them without saying a word to them; but if they strike you," Dostie concluded, "kill them."[34]

32. *GJR*, 8; *HSCR*, 312, 476, 478; *MCR*, 194, 226, 279–80. Tilton testified that Dostie's speech was much more incendiary than recounted here, but Tilton's testimony conflicts with that of R. L. Shelley, a reporter for the *New York Tribune*, who also listened to Dostie's speech. Even the newspaper reports the following day, which were highly critical of the rally, failed to corroborate Tilton's accusations regarding Dostie's intemperate language. These contradictions coupled with Tilton's excitable appearance and manner during his testimony led the military commission to discount his report (*MCR*, 39).
33. *HSCR*, 1, 32, 291–92.
34. *HSCR*, 38–39, 66. Dostie's remarks were reported independently by two witnesses, William Henry Hire and Stephen F. Fish, both of whom were supporters of the convention. Hire and Fish's uncle W. R. Fish were members. The quotation in the text is from Stephen Fish's testimony. Hire's account was more succinct. "Now, friends, go peaceably home; go orderly; do not disturb anybody; but if anybody disturbs you, kill him!"

5

Not More Than Half a Million Will Survive

REPORTS of the Friday night rally were in all of the papers Saturday morning. "The Radical Mob . . . Threatens and Thunders," read a headline in the *New Orleans Times*. The article portrayed the assembly as "a large crowd of those who aspire to become American citizens without distinction of color." The leaders were described as "the most uncharitable set of white men it has been our ill fortune to look upon for many a day," and the various speeches were characterized as "embittered elaboration," "a tirade of abuse," and "drivellings." Another New Orleans newspaper termed the speakers "virulent and abusive," noting that their language was "marked by coarse and emphatic invective." The *New Orleans Daily Picayune* described the participants as "extreme fanatics" who "entertained the most radical political views. . . . The proceedings last night astonished every good citizen and thinking man," the paper reported, "and the sentiments uttered by various speakers alarmed the whole community." The *Daily Picayune* condemned Dr. Dostie especially for his remarks on the steps of City Hall.[1]

Although the account in the *Daily Picayune* concerning Dostie's comments

1. *New Orleans Times*, July 28, 1866; *New Orleans Bee*, July 28, 1866; *New Orleans Daily Picayune*, July 28, 1866.

was probably accurate, the newspaper lied when it reported that speakers at the rally had urged blacks to arm themselves on Monday to defend the convention. In reality, some of the speakers had asked the crowd to stay away, not wanting to give the police an excuse for interfering with the meeting. But the conservative press in New Orleans was not interested in honesty and continued to rely on half-truths and hyperbole to fan the flames of racial unrest.[2]

Racial tensions in New Orleans had been on the rise since May 1862, when Union troops occupied the city. One reason for the escalation was Benjamin F. Butler's decision to organize fugitive slaves into regiments of black soldiers. It was bad enough that slaves had fled the plantations for a life of idleness in the city, white New Orleanians complained. Now the "Beast" was arming them. It was tantamount, they thought, to inciting an insurrection.[3]

It did not take long for confrontations between black soldiers and white citizens to spark antagonism on both sides. Many of these incidents centered around the city's streetcars. New Orleans had a system of segregated public transportation. Streetcars for blacks were marked with a large star, and black soldiers resented having to stand on the banquette waiting for an overcrowded "star car," while cars half full of whites rolled by. The white colonel of a black regiment tried to convince the city to put more star cars on the street, but to no avail. In September 1862, the *Daily Picayune* reported that several black soldiers had boarded a streetcar reserved for whites only. When the driver told them to get off, the soldiers punched him and attempted to break open the ticket box. Four weeks later, another black soldier was arrested for pulling a pistol on a streetcar and threatening to shoot the driver.[4]

By 1864, reports of crimes committed by black men in uniform became almost routine reading in the New Orleans press. In January, for example, four black soldiers were arrested for robbing a white man of $100 and beating him

2. *HSCR*, 350, 376, 478; Rable, *But There Was No Peace*, 48, 57.

3. *New Orleans Daily Picayune*, July 9, October 13, 25, 1863, January 5, February 13, March 23, April 1, May 13, 1864; Ripley, *Slaves and Freedmen*, 183; Tunnell, *Crucible of Reconstruction*, 71; [W. C. Corsan], *Two Months in the Confederate States, Including a Visit to New Orleans Under the Dominion of General Butler* (London: Richard Bentley, 1863), 39–40. For more on the reaction of white New Orleanians to black soldiers in the Union army, see "From Our Special Correspondent," *New York Times*, October 1, 1862.

4. "To the Free Colored People of New Orleans," *New Orleans Daily Delta*, November 9, 1862; *New Orleans Daily Picayune*, September 9, 23, 24, 1862, October 23, 1862; William F. Messner, "The Federal Army and Blacks in the Department of the Gulf, 1862–1865" (Ph.D. dissertation, University of Wisconsin, 1972), 75.

senseless. One week later, another black soldier was sentenced to life imprisonment for threatening and then robbing a white woman.[5]

The Union army was demobilized at the end of the war and most of the white troops were sent home. Black regiments, however, were retained for garrison duty throughout the South. Reports of crimes committed by these soldiers escalated the anger and fear of white New Orleanians, who resented having to have to live in the shadow of a black army of occupation.

Several such reports appeared in the New Orleans press at the end of the war. One of the first occurred on the Fourth of July, when, according to the *Daily True Delta*, a black soldier went into a grocery store in Carrollton and asked for a bottle of liquor. The store owner refused to sell it to the man and ordered him out of the store. The soldier left but returned a short time later with several of his friends, who proceeded to beat the store owner and help themselves to the liquor. When the store owner's wife tried to intervene, they knocked her down and left.[6]

The murder of a local medical doctor in Carrollton three months later further escalated racial tensions. It was reported that Dr. Octavius Trezevant and Judge Scott were taking an evening walk when they came upon a black soldier beating a black woman near the railroad depot. The two white men brusquely told the man to desist and continued their stroll. Several minutes later, they walked past the spot again on their way home. The soldier, Sergeant Fortune Wright, approached the two men, walking with a drunken gait. Dr. Trezevant continued on his way, but Judge Scott exchanged words with Wright. Wright pulled a large bowie knife and lunged at Scott, who warded off the thrust with his cane. Dr. Trezevant came to the aid of his friend and hit Wright with his walking stick. The soldier turned and stuck Dr. Trezevant in the side, wounding the doctor fatally.[7]

A racial incident of even larger proportions shattered the quiet of Christmas Day 1865. Two black men got into a fight outside a church in which a Christmas service was being held. A policeman intervened, and a large crowd of black churchgoers gathered around the officer when the two men resisted

5. *New Orleans Daily Picayune*, January 13, 20, 1864.

6. "The Negro Riot," *New Orleans Daily True Delta*, July 8, 1866. For example, in February a drunken black soldier assaulted several whites with a bayonet (*New Orleans Daily Crescent*, February 14, 1866). In July, a young white girl precipitated a riot when she uttered a racial slur while watching a black political procession (*New Orleans Daily Crescent*, July 7, 1866).

7. *New Orleans Daily Crescent*, October 24, 1865; *New Orleans Daily True Delta*, October 26, 1865, February 9, 16, March 3, 1866; *New Orleans Times*, March 3, 1866; *New Orleans Tribune*, March 9, 1866.

his intervention. Frightened, the police officer blew his whistle to summon help. Several policemen and white citizens came to his assistance. A scuffle ensued, and before it was over more than thirty blacks had been arrested and carted off to jail.[8]

The Christmas disturbance fueled rumors of an impending black insurrection on New Year's Day 1866, the third anniversary of the Emancipation Proclamation. The rumor was widespread throughout the South and increased the suspicion with which whites regarded their former slaves. Although the holiday passed uneventfully, the fear of racial unrest lingered beneath the surface.[9]

Sergeant Fortune Wright was scheduled to be executed for the murder of Dr. Trezevant on March 2, 1866. The case had continued to create interest throughout the winter because the date of the hanging had been delayed four times by appeals for a reprieve from Union army officers to President Johnson. When Johnson finally decided that he would not interfere, Wright was escorted to the scaffold at the parish prison. The event attracted several thousand spectators who filled the streets around the jail.[10]

"Farewell friends," Fortune Wright shouted as the cord supporting the drop was cut. Wright's body fell six feet, but the noose slipped over his chin and tightened around his forehead, leaving the prisoner suspended in midair. It was a new rope, and for some reason the hangman had failed to grease the knot. Although the jerk at the end of the fall caused Wright to black out, he was still alive. The attending surgeon checked his pulse and ordered Wright's body lowered to the ground and carried back up the steps to be hung a second time. The trap was sprung, and again the noose failed to tighten, but this time the rope caught Wright under his chin. After a few convulsive throes, Wright stopped breathing. The body hung for nearly an hour before it was cut down.[11] Presumably, many of the white spectators who witnessed the event thought that Fortune Wright had gotten just what he deserved.

8. *New Orleans Daily True Delta*, December 26, 27, 1865; *New Orleans Daily Picayune*, December 28, 1865.

9. Dan T. Carter, *When the War Was Over: The Failure of Self-Reconstruction in the South, 1865–1867* (Baton Rouge: Louisiana State University Press, 1985), 194–95. On New Year's Day, freedmen on the plantations "demeaned themselves in an orderly and peaceful manner," one newspaper reported ("Freedmen on the Plantations," *New Orleans Daily Picayune*, January 5, 1866).

10. *New Orleans Daily True Delta*, March 3, 1866; *New Orleans Times*, March 3, 1866.

11. *New Orleans Daily True Delta*, March 3, 1866; *New Orleans Times*, March 3, 1866; *New Orleans Tribune*, March 9, 1866.

Three weeks later, the *Daily Southern Star* reported another racial incident in Carrollton. On Sunday evening, March 25, a group of young, drunken white men was making its way along Front Street. A black man who had also been drinking came upon the party and tried to force his way through, muttering that he could "whip any white son of a bitch in Carrollton." The white boys retorted with curses, and when the black man continued his taunts, they responded with kicks and blows. A large number of blacks witnessing the dispute from a tenement house nearby rushed out into the street. A general free-for-all followed, with white citizens joining in the fracas. Several white soldiers from a Union infantry regiment also pitched in. It was a serious affair that left many wounded on both sides. Three blacks were killed, and the city of Carrollton shut up for the rest of the night when hotels, barrooms, and groceries closed their doors tight.[12]

The report of this incident crystallized the attitudes of most whites in New Orleans regarding race relations during the spring and early summer of 1866. If blacks continued to agitate for civil rights, a war between the races was inevitable. "Let professors and editors who stimulate the unhappy tendency of affairs, reflect on the consequences to society of demanding social and political equality for the negro," the *Daily Southern Star* warned. Noting that soldiers from Vermont had joined in the fight on the side of the whites, the *Star* predicted that racial loyalty would override regional differences resulting from the Civil War. "They [advocates for black civil rights] may excite him [the black man] to fight for it, but in that fight he will have to encounter not only all the Southern soldiers, but a powerful reinforcement of Northern men not yet prepared for the amalgamation of races."[13]

The zenith of journalistic sensationalism occurred on Saturday, July 28, the morning after the rally at the Mechanics' Institute. "A Negro Attempts to Violate a White Woman," read the headline. The story was almost three weeks old but still received space on the front page.[14]

The *Daily Crescent* reported that a black man about forty years old named William Yancey had approached two white women in Coliseum Square "and conducted himself with offensive familiarity." Both women ordered him to leave, but Yancey refused. They kept walking, and he followed. "All I want is a white wife," he was reported as saying. "I have money enough to support

12. "Riot in Carrollton—Conflict of the Races," *New Orleans Daily Southern Star*, March 27, 1866.

13. "The Irrepressible Conflict," *New Orleans Daily Southern Star*, March 28, 1866.

14. *New Orleans Daily Crescent*, July 28, 1866.

one, and I will go to St. Louis to get one." "Go away," one of the women demanded. Yancey grabbed her by the shoulder and pushed her, she claimed. "I don't want you old bitch. I want this pretty girl," he said, turning to the other. The second woman shrieked and struggled as Yancey grabbed her by the wrist. A policeman in the vicinity heard the shouts and came running. Although Yancey let go and took off, the officer caught up with him and took him to jail. This report in the *Daily Crescent*, coming as it did two days before the convention was scheduled to reconvene, served only to heighten tensions in a city already satiated with racial unrest.[15]

The doctrine of white supremacy was the foundation on which opposition to elevating the social and economic status of blacks in Louisiana was based. Most white southerners believed that the genetic characteristics of the black race made its advancement impossible. Rather than advance, many whites predicted that the black race would die out now that it was not cared for by a system of slavery. "We may reasonably conjecture that within the next decade of ten years, two and half millions will have perished, and within the next decade not more than half a million will survive," the *New Orleans Daily Bee* reported in a front-page article in January 1866.[16]

One of the most vocal proponents of this prediction was a nationally known physician and ethnologist from Mobile, Alabama, Josiah C. Nott. Basing his beliefs on his estimates of the cranium capacities of different races, Nott advanced an elaborate theory arguing that blacks had developed no further in intellectual ability than human beings at the time of the Egyptian civilization. "The physical and civil history of the negro proves that he never has lived, and never can live, in any other condition than that in which he has been placed," Nott wrote in regard to slavery. "The Negro rarely thinks of the future," he continued, "and learns little from experience." Nott was convinced that the black race in the South was certain to perish from disease and starvation. Given this perspective, an economy based on free black labor was bound to fail.[17]

15. Almost sixty years later, John Smith Kendall, a conservative newspaper editor, attributed much of the increase in racial tension to this report (*History of New Orleans*, 3 vols. [Chicago: Lewis, 1922], 1:307).

16. "John M. Bell on the Future of the Negro Race in the United States," *New Orleans Daily Bee*, January 16, 1866.

17. Reginald Horsman, *Josiah Nott of Mobile: Southerner, Physician, and Racial Theorist* (Baton Rouge: University of Louisiana Press, 1987), 1–3; John S. Haller, *Outcasts from Evolution: Scientific Attitudes of Racial Inferiority, 1859–1900* (Urbana: University of Illinois Press, 1971),

Whites in New Orleans looked to the record of emancipated labor in Haiti for evidence to support their pessimistic prediction. Emancipation had come to Haiti in the 1790s when the slaves revolted against their French masters. It was a bloody revolution; thousands of whites were killed, and the remainder fled into exile, many to New Orleans. The black slaves of Haiti proved to be formidable fighters, defeating armies from France and England and thereby establishing the hemisphere's second independent nation. But years of fighting had laid waste to the countryside, and a repressive labor system coupled with the need to maintain a large standing army resulted in a subsistence-oriented economy. By the 1830s, sugar production in Haiti had virtually come to a standstill. The violence, the economic collapse, and the corruption of the black Haitian regime were not lost on whites who believed the same thing would happen in Louisiana if they did not take steps to abort the process.[18]

The revolution in Haiti was not the only experience with emancipated labor in the hemisphere from which white New Orleanians could draw. In 1833, the British Crown freed the slaves in all of its far-flung empire. The largest number of emancipations was in Jamaica, which had 311,000 slaves. Jamaica was a sugar-exporting colony, and so the Jamaican experience could be compared directly to Louisiana.

The British authorities in Jamaica attempted to make the transition from slave to free labor by enforcing an apprenticeship system that bound former slaves to the land for six years at low wages and severe restrictions. When their term was up in the late 1830s, former slaves fled the plantations, preferring self-sufficiency on small plots of land. Just as in Haiti, sugar production fell.[19]

The worst fears of whites in Louisiana regarding the degeneracy of the black race and the futility of using free blacks for labor were confirmed in early November 1865, when news reached New Orleans of a massacre in Jamaica. Disturbed by the increasing number of squatters, white planters had turned to the courts to enforce trespassing laws. The resultant increase in racial tensions during the 1850s and 1860s erupted at Morant Bay on October 11, 1865, when a mob of blacks stormed the local court and butchered the magistrate and seventeen other whites with cutlasses and machetes. "Greatest alarm prevailing [the] whites" of Jamaica, the *Daily Southern Star* reported. Within days, the mail packets brought newspapers from New York, which provided

---

79–84; J. C. Nott, "Climates of the South in Their Relations to White Labor," *De Bow's Review* 1 (February 1866): 166–67.

18. Carter, *When the War Was Over*, 154; Eric Foner, *Nothing but Freedom: Emancipation and Its Legacy* (Baton Rouge: Louisiana State University Press, 1983), 11–12.

19. Foner, *Nothing but Freedom*, 14–20.

more specific information. The details were gruesome: an inspector's body mutilated, a clergyman's tongue cut out, and the magistrate's fingers snipped off before he died. If whites in Louisiana needed conclusive evidence of the failure of emancipated labor, newspaper reports of the massacre in Morant Bay provided it.[20]

20. Geoffrey Dutton, *The Hero as Murderer: The Life of Edward John Eyre, Australian Explorer and Governor of Jamaica, 1815–1901* (London: William Collins, 1967), 267–73; Foner, *Nothing but Freedom*, 24–27; *New York Times*, November 6, 1866; *New Orleans Daily Southern Star*, November 1, 1865.

6

Please Instruct Me at Once by Telegram

MAJOR GENERAL Philip H. Sheridan was the military commander in charge of Louisiana, Texas, Mississippi, and Florida. A no-nonsense professional soldier, Sheridan had not been a friend of Unionists in general and proponents of black suffrage in particular since coming to New Orleans the year before. "Those who represented themselves as Union men are no better than others," he had remarked.[1]

Sheridan was concerned that reconvening the constitutional convention might provoke a riot. "If the convention assembles and there is any disturbance," Sheridan had told Edward Durell in June when the judge had asked for military protection for the meeting, "I will disperse the mob and the convention and treat them both alike." Noting that the convention might give blacks the right to vote, Durell asked Sheridan whether he would protect them at the polls. No, Sheridan told the jurist. It was impossible; he did not have enough troops. But despite his concern, Sheridan was not even in New Orleans on Saturday, two days before the convention was scheduled to reconvene. He was on a trip to Texas to inspect troops stationed along the Rio Grande.[2]

1. *OR*, 48: pt. 2, 1087; *HSCR*, 85.
2. *HSCR*, 262–63, 347.

Assuming command in Sheridan's place was Absalom Baird. Baird's main responsibility was the Freedmen's Bureau in Louisiana. The Freedmen's Bureau had been established in 1864 to oversee the transformation of slaves into free men following emancipation. Its purpose was "to lessen the shock communicated to the people by the sudden change of the condition of freedom of the four millions slave population in the South," as the bureau's chief, General Oliver O. Howard, termed it. Normally, Baird reported directly to Howard in Washington. But Baird was also the second-ranking Union officer in New Orleans and thus assumed command when Sheridan departed for Texas.[3]

Before leaving, Sheridan had given Baird specific instructions not to place any soldiers around the Mechanics' Institute to avoid giving the appearance that the army was supporting the convention. Instead, Union troops should be kept in their barracks. The army should be used only in the case of a civil disturbance, Sheridan emphasized.[4]

That was the situation when Colonel A. P. Field, a local attorney who had spoken at the rally Friday evening, arrived at Baird's headquarters Saturday morning to tell the general of rumors that the local authorities planned to interfere with the convention when it reconvened on Monday. After a brief discussion, Baird told Field that he had been in communication with the mayor, John T. Monroe, and that he did not believe Monroe planned to disturb the meeting.[5]

Baird discovered that he was wrong when Mayor Monroe and Lieutenant Governor Albert Voorhies showed up at his headquarters shortly after Colonel Field left. This was the first time Baird had met the lieutenant governor. A member of the Louisiana Supreme Court before the war, the thirty-seven-year-old jurist had attended law school at Transylvania University in Lexington, Kentucky. He had been admitted to the bar at the age of nineteen and was active in the Democratic Party before the war. During the war, Voorhies had served as the Confederate judge advocate general for the Trans-Mississippi Department.[6]

Voorhies did most of the talking. Unaware that Wells had returned to the city Friday afternoon, Voorhies told Baird that he had been unable to contact

3. *HSCR* 441; "Gen. Howard Defines the Object of His Visit," *New Orleans Times*, November 6, 1865. The bureau's official name was the Bureau of Refugees, Freedmen, and Abandoned Lands.

4. *HSCR*, 350.

5. *HSCR*, 442.

6. Conrad, ed., *Dictionary of Louisiana Biography*, 2: 815–16; *New Orleans Daily Picayune*, January 21, 1913.

the governor in regard to the convention. Believing that Wells was still on his plantation near Alexandria, Voorhies had decided to act on his own.[7]

Mayor Monroe broke in. He wanted the city police to arrest members of the convention when they reconvened. The lieutenant governor objected. Let the grand jury of Orleans Parish assemble after the meeting took place, Voorhies suggested, and issue writs of arrest for the sheriff to serve. Baird disagreed. "Tell the Sheriff not to do it," he informed the lieutenant governor. "These people have a right to meet; if you arrest them, it will be a violation of their rights." Voorhies contended that the assembly was unlawful. Its object, he argued, was to subvert the state government. Baird held his ground, for he considered the dispute to be political in nature and believed that the Democrats were trying to use the courts to gain an advantage over their opponents. If the sheriff detained the delegates to the convention, Baird announced, he would release them and arrest the sheriff instead.[8]

Voorhies got the message. The lieutenant governor agreed that the sheriff would not serve the writs issued by the grand jury without Baird's permission. Baird then asked whether the convention would complete its business in one day. Voorhies said no, which pleased Baird. There was no reason for haste; the delegates could be arrested on Tuesday or any subsequent day if necessary. Baird added that he would telegraph Washington to get definite instructions as to how to proceed. Voorhies told Baird about the telegram he had received from Rozier following the emissary's talk with President Johnson. Voorhies had already sent a telegram to the president, asking him to confirm what he had told Rozier about keeping the military from interfering with local authorities. Baird repeated that he would telegraph the secretary of war, Edwin M. Stanton, to determine the administration's stance regarding the convention.[9]

The meeting lasted almost an hour. In the end, the three men agreed that the convention should be allowed to assemble unless Baird received instructions to the contrary from Washington. If Baird was ordered to allow the sheriff to arrest the delegates, it would be done without disorder or violence. Voorhies promised that the sheriff would go by himself to the meeting and call on the members to submit themselves for arrest without force being used. Before Monroe and Voorhies left, Baird made one last point. If the army had to intervene to put down a riot, the consequences would be disastrous to Louisiana's efforts to be readmitted to the Union. Voorhies and Monroe agreed with

7. *HSCR*, 442; *MCR* 168, 268.
8. *GJR*, 12–13; *HSCR*, 442–43; *MCR*, 268, 273.
9. *New Orleans Times*, July 30, 1866; *HSCR*, 219, 236, 443; *MCR*, 268.

Baird's assessment and offered to place notices in the city newspapers asking persons not associated with the convention to avoid the streets in the vicinity of the Mechanics' Institute on Monday.[10]

As soon as the lieutenant governor and mayor left his office, Baird wrote out a telegram to the secretary of war in Washington.[11]

> Hon. Edwin M. Stanton, Secretary of War:
>
> A Convention has been called, with the sanction of the Governor Wells to meet here on Monday. The Lieutenant-Governor and city authorities think it is unlawful, and propose to break it up by arresting the delegates. I have given no orders on the subject, but have warned the parties that I could not countenance or permit such action without instructions to that effect from the President. Please instruct me at once by telegram.
>
> A. BAIRD,
> Brevet Major General Commanding

On his way back to City Hall, Mayor Monroe stopped by the office of the chief of police, Thomas E. Adams, to discuss plans for handling the situation on Monday. Monroe was not afraid to use force. A distant relative of President James Monroe and a veteran of the Texas War of Independence, the forty-three-year-old Monroe began his career as a stevedore on the New Orleans docks, where he organized gangs of longshoremen. He joined the strongly anti-immigrant American Party in 1858 and won election to the post of assistant alderman from the city's largely Anglo-American First District. Realizing that the party's anti-Catholic doctrine was a political liability in Louisiana, Monroe struck out on his own in 1860 and ran for mayor with the support of the city's immigrant and creole workers. He won.[12]

Once in office, Monroe moved quickly to consolidate his power. Formalizing the strong-arm tactics he had employed successfully against immigrants as a veteran of the Know-Nothing movement, Monroe stepped up the enforcement of old laws designed to circumscribe the freedoms of the city's black population. The mayor's newly reconstituted police force arrested slaves living

10. Voorhies (*HSCR*, 236), Baird (*HSCR*, 443).

11. Baird (*HSCR*, 442–43); Baird's telegram is also in *MCR*, 101.

12. *HSCR*, 112; *MCR*, 113; Mary Jacqueline Herbert, "John T. Monroe: Race, Politics, and the Police in New Orleans, 1858–1866" (M.A. University of New Orleans, 1991), 2–3. Monroe was elected by a majority of 1,734 out of 7,593 votes cast (W. Darrell Overdyke, *The Know-Nothing Party in the South* [Baton Rouge: Louisiana State University Press, 1950], 291–92).

independently in New Orleans and intimidated members of the prominent free black community by accusing them of promoting abolitionism and urging black bondsmen to revolt. The white populace of New Orleans squealed with delight. "We are glad to see the police acting with so much vigor and promptness," the *Daily Picayune* proclaimed. "Too much encouragement cannot be given to the officers who understand and carry out their duty in such a manner." They had found a mayor who stood for law and order.[13]

Monroe had just been reelected as the Confederate mayor of New Orleans when the Union fleet steamed past the forts guarding the Mississippi River in April 1862. Benjamin F. Butler attempted to gain Monroe's cooperation when he occupied the city. At first the mayor went along, but he soon found it difficult to cooperate as Butler's grip on the city tightened. Eventually, Butler had Monroe arrested and thrown in the dungeon at Fort Jackson. When Nathaniel P. Banks replaced Butler in December 1862, he offered to release Monroe if the mayor took the oath of allegiance to the United States government. Monroe refused and sat in a prison cell for another nine months until he was freed under the condition that he not return to the city. Monroe crossed the lines and waited out the war in Mobile, Alabama, finally returning to New Orleans in 1865.[14]

Monroe ran for mayor a third time in the municipal elections of March 1866 and was elected with 52 percent of the vote. Hugh Kennedy, Wells's appointee and the outgoing mayor, was shocked to discover that Monroe had been reelected. Kennedy had wired President Johnson for instructions. "We have no information showing that the election was not regular, or that the individual who has been elected cannot qualify," Johnson responded. "In the absence of such information, the presumption is that the election has been [according] to law, and that the person elected [Monroe] can take the oath of allegiance and loyalty required."[15]

Kennedy protested. "The mayor elected was mayor under the confederate authorities, imprisoned by General Butler for aggravated hostility to re-establishment of national authority, and finally voluntarily left Union lines for the

13. Herbert, "John T. Monroe," 17–23; "Prompt Work," *New Orleans Daily Picayune,* September 5, 1860.

14. *HSCR,* 131; *New Orleans Daily Picayune,* May 22, 1862; *New Orleans Daily Delta,* June 14, July 18, 1862; *New Orleans Daily True Delta,* December 25, 1862; *New Orleans Daily Crescent,* May 15, 1866; "Memorandum," May 19, 1862, in Butler, *Private and Official Correspondence,* 1:498; Herbert, "John T. Monroe," 24–26.

15. *New Orleans Daily Picayune,* March 4, 7, 8, 1866; *HSCR,* 518. The vote was 3,469 for Monroe, 3,158 for his opponent, Joseph Moore (*New Orleans Daily Crescent,* March 14, 1866).

confederacy, peremptorily refusing to take an oath of allegiance." Kennedy went on to tell the president that the new mayor had not been pardoned following the war and that "Union sentiment is unanimously against him." Johnson declined to intervene and even issued Monroe a pardon when the mayor-elect traveled to Washington to plead his case. Gratified by the president's support, Monroe returned to New Orleans and assumed office on May 14, just ten weeks before the convention was scheduled to reconvene.[16]

Now that he was back in office, Monroe had no intention of letting the advocates of black suffrage preempt his authority. Monroe told Adams to make sure his men were armed. Although police officers were not supposed to carry firearms, Chief Adams did not attempt to enforce the ordinance. As a result, many of the police had purchased revolvers with their own money and carried them on their beats. The mayor would try to find arms for the police who did not have them. The entire police force, including the night shift, was to report to their stations Monday morning in anticipation of trouble.[17]

Twenty or more prominent citizens met in Mayor Monroe's office on Saturday evening to discuss how to handle the meeting of the convention scheduled for Monday. All of the major state officials were there with the exception of Governor Wells. Chief Adams, Sheriff Harry T. Hays, and Judge Edmund Abell were present, as was Frank J. Herron, a former major general in the Union army whose opinion Mayor Monroe valued. In addition, there were several prominent citizens, including Richard Taylor, a former lieutenant general in the Confederate army.[18]

The meeting started with Monroe reading a letter he had written to General Baird earlier that week: "A body of men claiming to belong to the convention of 1864, and whose avowed object is to subvert the present municipal and State government will, I learn, assemble in this city Monday next." Citing his authority as mayor to maintain the public peace and tranquillity, Monroe informed Baird that it was his intention to disperse the members of "this unlawful assembly . . . *provided* they meet without the sanction of the military authorities." Monroe then asked Baird to inform him whether he objected to the meeting so that he could "act accordingly."[19]

16. *HSCR*, 518; *New Orleans Daily Crescent*, May 9, 15, 1866.
17. *HSCR*, 111–12, 201, 286.
18. *MCR*, 56; *GJR*, 16; Affidavit to Judge E. Heistand by R. King Cutler and other members of the convention, August 3, 1866, Letters Received by the Adjutant General's Office, 1861–70, RG 536, M-619, Roll 427, NA.
19. Monroe's letter to Baird, July 25, 1866, in *MCR*, 6–7, also 99.

Baird had responded on Thursday, and his reply was also read out loud. In it, Baird informed Monroe that he had been instructed to refrain from interfering with political activities occurring within the state. For that reason, he had declined a request to send troops to protect the meeting, assuming that the mayor and the police would maintain order. Anticipating what he had said to Monroe and Voorhies during their meeting that morning, Baird's letter stated that the delegates to the convention had the right to assemble and discuss matters concerning the state government. "If the assemblage in question has the legal right to remodel the State government," Baird argued, "it should be protected in so doing; if it has not, then its labors must be looked upon as a piece of harmless pleasantry, to which no one ought to object."[20]

After he finished reading Baird's letter, Monroe turned to Herron and asked for his opinion. Herron stated that he did not think that the municipal authorities had a right to interfere with the meeting. If the meeting was illegal, as Monroe believed, then the proper course was to let them reconvene and have the grand jury issue warrants for their arrest. Sheriff Hays could then take the warrants to Baird and to President Johnson, if needed, for their approval. In the meantime, Herron argued that the police should be used to protect the meeting to avoid civil disturbance that might be sparked by hotheads who wanted to disrupt the proceedings.[21]

One of those present objected to Herron's plan. "If I could have my way," he announced, "I would hang the members of the convention first and try them afterwards!" Others in the room spoke up against the man's wild talk. Sheriff Hays voiced his agreement with Herron's position. Lieutenant Governor Voorhies also agreed with Herron, for the former Union army general was proposing essentially the same arrangement he had worked out with Baird earlier that day.[22]

Despite the consensus not to interfere with the meeting, there was still the question of how to prevent a confrontation between the supporters of the convention and white citizens bent on disrupting the proceedings. Chief Adams voiced his opposition to sending his men in force to the Mechanics' Institute because it would give the appearance of supporting the convention. He was also concerned that a strong police presence might provoke a confrontation with black supporters of the meeting.[23]

20. Baird to Monroe, July 26, 1866, in *MCR*, 7, also 99–100.
21. *MCR*, 56.
22. *MCR*, 57.
23. *GJR*, 13.

Monroe agreed with Chief Adams and reminded him to keep his men in readiness at their station houses. Instead of sending policemen to protect the convention delegates, Monroe would issue a proclamation admonishing all persons not directly connected with the convention to keep away from the Mechanics' Institute on Monday. In his decree, Monroe would warn the citizens of New Orleans that a breach of the peace would give opponents of Johnson's Reconstruction policy ammunition and thus weaken the president's attempt to let Louisiana reconstruct itself. Monroe would also reassure the citizens that Johnson would not support the delegates or sustain any attempt they made to rewrite the constitution. The group accepted the mayor's proposal and adjourned, optimistic that trouble could be avoided.

7

To-morrow Will Be the Bloodiest Day

MOSES FOX, a sixty-seven-year-old white carpenter, left his room on Bienville Street on Sunday morning and went to the Tremé market to get a newspaper. On his way home, Fox ran into Officer Gallaway, a policeman he had met while on jury duty. Naturally, their conversation turned to the convention on Monday. "Unless the Mayor withdraws the orders that he gave to the police yesterday," Gallaway remarked, "to-morrow will be the bloodiest day they ever had in the city of New Orleans."[1]

Fox was worried, for he had many friends who were involved with the convention. He set out for R. King Cutler's office at 19 Commercial Place between Camp and St. Charles, knowing that the people who supported the decision to reconvene the convention often met there. No one was at the office except Judge Ezra Heistand. Fox told Heistand what he had heard. Heistand told Fox to keep an eye on Gallaway but offered no encouragement. Fox then went to Cutler's house in Jefferson City, thinking that perhaps Governor Wells was in conference with Cutler regarding the convention.

---

1. *HSCR*, 200. Gallaway's name is spelled Gallway and Gallaway in the House Select Committee Report.

The governor could do something, Fox thought. Wells was not there, but Cutler was home.[2]

Cutler was not an extremist by nature, but the success of former secessionists at the polls had made him much more of a revolutionary than he had been two years earlier when the constitutional convention had met. In 1864, Cutler had defended the abolition of slavery on the purely pragmatic grounds that it would hasten the end of the war. By 1866, things had changed. "Rebels reign Supreme here," Cutler had written Senator Lyman Trumbull the previous December. "The rebel legislature now in session are about to elect two U.S. Senators in place of myself and Mr. Hahn," he complained. Faced with the loss of his Senate seat, which he had not been allowed to occupy but which he still held as a point of honor, Cutler traveled down the same road Wells, Hahn, and others associated with the Free State of Louisiana had followed. "If Congress would admit La, reserving the right to regulate the franchise of her people White and Black," he informed Trumbull, "there would be no danger in the future. This I know is a slight change of my base," he admitted, "but I love my Country and hate disloyalty—and if disfranchising traitors, and enfranchising loyal intelligent Negroes, will save my Country then I favor the measure, and it seems extremely doubtful if anything else will save Louisiana."[3]

Fox told Cutler of the threats. Cutler thanked Fox for the warning and told him that several members of the convention were going to meet at the Custom House Monday morning before the convention reconvened to discuss what actions they should take. Having done his duty, Fox returned home.[4]

Absalom Baird sat in his office waiting for Stanton's reply to the telegram he had sent the day before. The grandson of a surgeon in the Revolutionary Army and the great-grandson of a lieutenant in the French and Indian Wars, Baird had graduated ninth in his class of forty-three at West Point. After fighting the Seminoles in Florida, Baird taught mathematics at the Military Academy for six years before serving a tour of duty on the Texas frontier.[5]

2. Fox refers to "Judge Hawkins" in his testimony. The name is probably a transcription error. The only other reference to a "Judge Hawkins" during this period occurs in the *New Orleans Daily Crescent* (July 28, 1866), where he is identified as speaking at the Friday night rally. It was Judge Heistand who spoke on that occasion (*HSCR*, 1). Cutler's house was on Napoleon Avenue at the corner of Jersey Street.

3. Cutler to Trumbull, August 29, December 6, 1865, Lyman Trumbull Papers, LC.

4. Fox, *HSCR*, 200.

5. Ezra J. Warner, *Generals in Blue: Lives of the Union Commanders* (Baton Rouge: Louisiana State University Press, 1964), 15.

Baird had begun the Civil War as a staff officer but rose to command a division in the Army of the Tennessee. He had fought at Chattanooga, Chickamauga, and Atlanta, where he won a Congressional Medal of Honor for gallantry. Baird led his division with Sherman on the march through Georgia and was present at the final surrender of General Joseph E. Johnston in North Carolina. With the war at an end, Baird's experience as a staff officer made him a good choice to head up the Freedmen's Bureau in Louisiana. He had just turned forty-two when he reached the Crescent City in November 1865 to assume his new duties.[6]

The secretary of war had received the telegram Saturday morning, but Baird's request for instructions placed Stanton in an awkward position. Stanton was well aware of Johnson's policy regarding the reconstruction of the South. Had he shown the telegram to the president, Stanton knew that Johnson would order Baird to support the local authorities. But Stanton did not wish to cross the president openly by ordering Baird to protect the convention. Seeing no easy solution to his dilemma, Stanton decided to sit on it.[7]

While waiting for Stanton to reply, Baird did what he could to prepare his troops for Monday. The force he had at his disposal consisted of two regiments of infantry and a battery of light artillery. One of the regiments was a

6. Joseph G. Dawson, *Army Generals and Reconstruction*, 37; John A. Baird, Jr., *Profile of a Hero: The Story of Absalom Baird, His Family, and the American Military Tradition* (Philadelphia: Dorrance, 1977), 154–57; *New Orleans Daily Picayune*, November 12, 1865.

7. Secretary of War, *Message of the President of the United States and the Report of the Committee on Military Affairs, Etc., in Regard to the Suspension of Hon. E. M. Stanton* (Washington, D.C.: U.S. Government Printing Office, 1868), 8–9; Benjamin P. Thomas and Harold M. Hyman, *Stanton: The Life and Times of Lincoln's Secretary of War* (New York: Knopf, 1962), 495–97; Fletcher Pratt, *Stanton: Lincoln's Secretary of War* (New York: Norton, 1953), 445. Baird's telegram arrived at the War Department shortly after 10 P.M. Saturday (James E. Sefton, *The United States Army and Reconstruction, 1865–1877* [Baton Rouge: Louisiana State University Press, 1967], 85). Johnson did not see Baird's telegram until several days after the riot had occurred (W. G. Moore, "Notes of Colonel W. G. Moore, Private Secretary to President Johnson, 1866–1868," *American Historical Review* 19 [October 1913]: 102). Stanton was later accused of purposely withholding the information to discredit the president because of the resultant violence. This interpretation, however, is generally out of favor (Patrick W. Riddleberger, *1866: The Critical Year Revisited* [Carbondale: Southern Illinois University Press, 1979], 191–94; Sefton, *United States Army and Reconstruction*, 87; Thomas and Hyman, *Stanton*, 497). Baird came in for his share of the criticism as well. Why had he not wired the president directly? Baird later explained that the usual mode of communication with Washington was through the adjutant general, which necessitated some delay. Baird testified that he had violated standard operating procedures already by telegraphing Stanton and did not feel justified passing over the secretary of war to communicate directly with the president (Riddleberger, *1866*, 192; *HSCR*, 451).

regular army unit, the 1st United States Infantry. The 1st Infantry had 708 men and 18 officers present for duty at the Jackson Barracks about three miles below the city. The battery of light artillery was stationed there as well. Baird could also call on a black regiment, the 81st Infantry, United States Colored Troops, which had 580 men and 20 officers present for duty. The 81st Infantry was stationed closer to the Mechanics' Institute than the 1st, but Baird was hesitant to use this regiment because of racial tensions in the city. Nevertheless, he decided to put both regiments on alert and ordered a steamboat at Jackson Barracks to maintain a head of steam all day Monday in case it was called upon to ferry the 1st Infantry to the city. Baird also ordered a tug to be kept ready at the city wharf to provide rapid communication with the barracks.[8]

Mayor Monroe was also preparing for the reconvening of the convention the next day. He needed men to keep the crowd under control, and his first choice for this work was the police force. Monroe could count on the police, for they were former Confederates like himself. He had seen to that in May when he assumed office by discharging police officers who had served in the Union army and replacing them with Confederate veterans. Although Monroe had retained a handful of former Union soldiers whose special skills made them difficult to replace, about two-thirds of the 499-man force had served in either the Confederate army or the Louisiana militia during the war. Even though they were accustomed to army discipline, the mayor's new police force had no training in law enforcement.[9]

8. July 1866 return for 1st United States Infantry, Returns from Regular Army Infantry Regiments, June 1821–December 1916, NA; July 1866 return for Battery "K," 1st U.S. Artillery, Returns from U.S. Military Posts, 1800–1916, Jackson Barracks, La., February 1837–December 1869, NA; Inspection Report, 81st U.S.C. Infantry for the Month of July 1866, U.S. Colored Troops, Regimental Papers, 81st–84th U.S. Colored Inf., NA. The location of the 81st Infantry comes from Baird's testimony in *HSCR*, 443. Baird's order read: "Without the least apprehension of any disturbance tomorrow requiring military aid, the General Commanding desires you will keep your troops well in hand during the day and evening requiring all officers and men not on duty to remain within sound of the drums of the camp ready to move at short notice, should they be called upon by order from there or superior headquarters" (1st Lt. Nathaniel Burbank to Lt. Col. G. C. Getchell, July 29, 1866, Letters Sent, Department of the Gulf, NA). See also *MCR*, 102, 274.

9. *HSCR*, 5, 67, 238, 394, 529; *MCR*, 277, 287; John Gibbons to N. P. Banks, July 30, 1866, Banks Collection; see also "Police Reorganization" [in German], *New Orleans Deutsche Zeitung*, May 29, 1866, and Vandal, "New Orleans Riot," 254–55. Although the first manual for policemen in New Orleans was issued in 1852, it was customary for new appointees to receive on-the-job training only (Rousey, *Policing the Southern City*, 95–96).

Former Confederates on the police force had a special interest in the proceedings on Monday. If the convention was successful, it might establish qualifications for public office that would prevent veterans of the Confederate army from serving as police officers. The prospect of losing a job, especially one paying $80 a month in a city where high unemployment was the rule, gave the police with rebel backgrounds an extra incentive to make sure that the convention did not reconvene.[10]

Some policemen knew just what to do to make sure the convention would fail. Veterans of the Know-Nothing movement before the war, these men had served as the bullies of the American Party. Called "thugs" by respectable citizens who considered them to represent "the low, ruffian, rowdy class, which all large cities have," they were political mercenaries who could be counted on to intimidate, beat, or even murder a man to keep him from voting. Monroe had used the thugs effectively during his previous terms as mayor and had called upon them again during the recent balloting in which he had been re-elected. They were his secret police, whom the black citizens in New Orleans despised and feared as "the worst kind of men generally."[11]

None of the thugs was more notorious than Lucien Adams. Adams's claim to fame was his use of strong-arm tactics on election days during the 1850s. At one point, he had to flee the city to avoid being tried for murder. Butler had thrown Adams in prison for sedition in 1862, but the bully had escaped prosecution when Butler was recalled. Lucien Adams's reputation was so odious that Chief Adams, who was no relation, had strongly opposed his being placed on the police force. But in May when the chief was suspended briefly for allowing citizens to carry concealed weapons, Monroe had appointed Lu-

10. *HSCR*, 409; "Policemen," *New Orleans Daily Picayune*, May 3, 1866. The 1864 constitution required police officers to be registered voters. Disfranchising former Confederate soldiers would thereby exclude them from serving on the force (Vandal, "New Orleans Riot," 143, 263 n. 45).

11. *HSCR*, 22, 42, 121, 494, 505; J. Madison Wells to Andrew Johnson, February 10, 1866, in *HSCR*, 520; "The Mayor and Police Corruption," *New Orleans Daily Picayune*, August 22, 1865; Overdyke, *Know-Nothing Party in the South*, 240–60; Leon Cyprian Soulé, *The Know Nothing Party in New Orleans: A Reappraisal* (Baton Rouge: Thomas J. Moran's Sons for the Louisiana Historical Association, 1961), 54–58, 72–73, 79–82, 95–102. Evidence that the thugs were up to their old tricks can be deduced from the circumstances surrounding the murder of John F. Gruber three days before the election (*New Orleans Daily Picayune*, March 27, 30, 1866), as well as the grand jury's report of April 3, 1866, published in the *New Orleans Daily Southern Star*, April 4, 1866. Confederate sympathizers claimed that there was a secret pro-Union club in the police force that attempted to coerce policemen to support the governor's slate of candidates ("Interference of the Police," *New Orleans Daily Picayune*, March 7, 1866).

cien Adams to the rank of sergeant. Now Adams commanded the First District substation on Pecanier (now Chippewa) Street.[12]

Mayor Monroe had yet another body of men he could summon to quell a disturbance if needed—the sheriff's department for Orleans Parish. The sheriff, Harry Thompson Hays, was a former brigadier general in the Confederate army. Hays also relied heavily on Confederate veterans for his deputies, especially those who had served under him in the Army of Northern Virginia. Although he did not have nearly the number of deputies that Chief Adams had in his force, Hays could also call on the Hays Brigade Relief Society if needed.[13]

The Hays Brigade Relief Society was one of several Confederate veterans' groups organized in New Orleans immediately after the war. Its purpose, at least publicly, was to commemorate the Confederate dead, to provide relief for widows and orphans, and to furnish mutual support. Groups like the Hays Brigade Relief Society were hardly secret; announcements of their meetings and charitable balls appeared in the newspapers. Nevertheless, they also served as a nucleus for a strike force that could respond quickly when called upon. Sheriff Hays sent out the word on Sunday, and some two hundred men, veterans of his old brigade, reported that evening to be sworn in as special deputies.[14]

Thomas Adams had first served as chief of police before the war under another mayor. He had been a conscientious chief in 1858, and eight years later Adams still believed that his primary duty was to ensure the peace. To that end, Adams had decided to keep his men out of sight as much as possible so as not to give the appearance of wanting to provoke a confrontation. Thus Adams was now faced with a problem. Because his men were being held in

12. *HSCR*, 96, 499; *MCR*, 270, 277. Thomas Adams's suspension lasted from May 16 to May 31, 1866 (*New Orleans Daily Crescent*, May 22, 1866). Among other things, Lucien Adams was involved in an incident in which a Unionist was tarred, feathered, and run out of town (*New Orleans Daily Delta*, November 1, 5, 1862).

13. Conrad, ed., *Dictionary of Louisiana Biography*, 1:386; *HSCR*, 84–86.

14. *HSCR*, 14, 25, 42, 520–21, 533; *New Orleans Daily Crescent*, May 18, June 4, 1866; *New Orleans Daily Picayune*, May 10, 1866; also see Wells's message to the special session of the legislature, November 29, 1865, printed in the *New Orleans Daily Picayune*, December 1, 1865; and Sheridan to J. A. Rawlins, June 5, 1866, Philip H. Sheridan Papers, LC. The constitution of the Washington Artillery Relief and Monumental Association appeared in the *New Orleans Daily Crescent* on May 22, 1866. Sheridan outlawed these societies (*New Orleans Daily Crescent*, July 23, 1866).

reserve, Adams needed a way to summon them quickly should trouble arise. Fortunately, the fire-police telegraph system provided a solution.[15]

The fire-police telegraph had been installed in 1859 by John N. Gamewell and Company of Camden, South Carolina, and was similar to systems in Boston, New York, and Philadelphia. The alarm system consisted of sixty-five signal stations—cast iron, cottage-shaped boxes attached to the sides of houses, telegraph poles, or gas lamps and connected to the central office in the First District police station behind City Hall by a circuit of telegraph lines stretched overhead between tall poles. Normally, these boxes were locked, but every watchman and policeman had a key. When a watchman spotted smoke, he ran to the nearest box, unlocked it, and turned a crank inside.[16]

Turning the crank sent a signal to the central station, indicating the district and box number from which the signal had come. The telegraph operator at the central station used a keyboard to activate any or all of the thirteen large alarm bells located strategically throughout the city, usually on the steeples of prominent churches. New Orleans was divided into nine fire districts. If the originating box was, for example, number five in district three, the alarm bells would strike three times. Using another control, the central operator could send a second command to all of the signal boxes in the appropriate district. This command would cause a small bell inside each box to tap out the location of the signal box from which the initial alarm was sounded (i.e., five times, in this example). Firemen were directed to the appropriate district by large alarm bells and, once there, to the location of the fire by listening to the small bell inside one of the signal boxes.[17]

At ten o'clock the superintendent of the telegraph system informed the

15. *MCR*, 114. Adams was a businessman and member of the state legislature before being appointed chief of police in 1858 by Mayor Gerard Stith (Dennis C. Rousey, *Policing the Southern City: New Orleans, 1805–1889* (Baton Rouge: Louisiana State University Press, 1996), 79). For a favorable assessment of Adams's character, see the testimony of a former Union army general, Lionel A. Sheldon, in *HSCR* (p. 281).

16. *The American Fire Alarm and Police Telegraph* (New Orleans: Clark and Brisbin, 1859), 3. Each signal box was also equipped with a telegraph key that enabled policemen on the beat to communicate directly with the central station. This capability had many practical uses, the most common of which was to report finding lost children. During 1865, the fire-police telegraph was used to locate 419 boys and 277 girls (*New Orleans Daily Southern Star*, February 4, 1866).

17. *New Orleans Daily True Delta*, March 27, 1860; *New Orleans Daily Crescent*, March 29, 1860; *New Orleans Times*, February 24, 1866; *American Fire Alarm*, 6; George H. Allen to Alderman Bosworth, January 3, 1867, Superintendent to the Board of Assistant Aldermen, March 29, 1867, both in City Council Reports of City Departments to the Board of Aldermen, 1866–69, City Archives, Louisiana Division, New Orleans Public Library.

chief engineer of the fire department that the signal for the police would be twelve strikes of the alarm bells. Since the city was divided into nine fire districts, a twelve-strike signal would not be confused with a real fire alarm, nor would it be confused with the fire department's general alarm, which was twenty strikes.

This would not be the first time the twelve-strike signal had been used. Four years earlier, while David G. Farragut bombarded the forts on each side of the Mississippi River south of the city, the twelve-strike signal had been adopted by the Confederate commander to summon the militia should the Union navy blast its way past the forts. Twelve strikes of the fire-police telegraph system in 1862 meant the fall of the city to the federal fleet and the coming of "Beast" Butler with his Yankee minions. When the police heard twelve strikes tomorrow, they would know what to do.[18]

Having arranged for the signal, Adams sent orders by messengers to the precinct stations to pull the night shift off the streets at midnight. Some were told to go home and rest, others were told to remain at the station house for the rest of the night. All were ordered to report for duty no later than eight o'clock the next morning. To protect the city through the night, Chief Adams ordered a handful of "extras," citizens who occasionally filled in for regular duty policemen when the need arose, to walk the beats of the night shift.[19]

18. *New Orleans Daily Delta*, January 19, 24, 1861; *HSCR*, 2, 79, 206; *MCR*, 67–68.
19. *HSCR*, 142, 204, 343; *MCR*, 155, 230, 276–77.

Absalom Baird, Major-General, U.S.
Army.
*From the Gil Barrett Collection. Courtesy of
the U.S.A.M.H.I.*

Dr. Anthony P. Dostie.
From Emily Hazen Reed, Life of A. P.
Dostie. *Courtesy of the Howard-Tilton
Memorial Library, Tulane University.*

Michael Hahn, Governor of the Free
State of Louisiana, 1864–65.
From Harper's Weekly, *March 26, 1864.*
Courtesy of the Historic New
Orleans Collection.

Rev. Jotham Warren Horton.
From In Memoriam. *Courtesy of the*
Howard-Tilton Memorial Library,
Tulane University.

John T. Monroe, Mayor of New Orleans, 1860–62, 1866–67. *From* Harper's Weekly, *August 25, 1866. Courtesy of Special Collections, LSU Libraries, Baton Rouge.*

J. Madison Wells, Governor of Louisiana, 1865–67. *From* Harper's Weekly, *November 11, 1865. Courtesy of Special Collections, LSU Libraries, Baton Rouge.*

The Mechanics' Institute.
Courtesy of Dr. Glen C. Cangelosi.

View of Canal Street toward the river from the corner of Canal and Carondolet streets, two blocks the intersection of Canal and Dryades.
From the Marshall Dunhum Photograph Album, Mss. 3241. Courtesy of the Louisiana and Lower Mississippi Valley Collections, LSU Libraries, Louisiana State University, Baton Rouge, La.

New Orleans City Hall, across the street from Lafayette Park.
From the Marshall Dunhum Photograph Album, Mss. 3241. Courtesy of the Louisiana and Lower Mississippi Valley Collections, LSU Libraries, Louisiana State University, Baton Rouge, La.

HARPER'S WEEKLY

A JOURNAL OF CIVILIZATION

Vol. X.—No. 504.]   NEW YORK, SATURDAY, AUGUST 25, 1866.   [SINGLE COPIES TEN CENTS.
$4.00 PER YEAR IN ADVANCE.

THE RIOT IN NEW ORLEANS—MURDER OF THE REV. MR. HORTON IN THE VESTIBULE OF THE MECHANICS' INSTITUTE.—SKETCHED BY DAVIS.—[SEE PAGE 535.]

The New Orleans riot was on the cover of the August 25, 1866, issue of *Harper's Weekly*. An article about the riot was illustrated with six additional images inside. The caption that appeared on the cover read "Murder of the Rev. Mr. Horton in the vestibule of the Mechanics' Institute." Although the illustration was not accurate (Horton was shot in the hall, not in the vestibule, and he sustained his fatal wounds after, not before, he was arrested), this issue of *Harper's Weekly* arrived in Northern homes just a few weeks before the important Congressional elections in November 1866.

From Harper's Weekly, *August 25, 1866. Courtesy of Special Collections, LSU Libraries, Baton Rouge.*

"The Freedmen's Procession marching to the Institute—the struggle for the flag."
From Harper's Weekly, *August 25, 1866. Courtesy of Special Collections, LSU Libraries, Baton Rouge.*

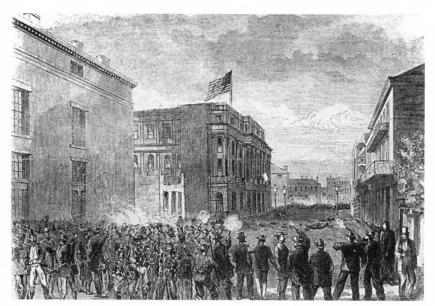

"Siege and assault of the convention by the police and citizens."
From Harper's Weekly, *August 25, 1866. Courtesy of Special Collections, LSU Libraries, Baton Rouge.*

"Murdering Negroes in the rear of Mechanics' Institute."
From Harper's Weekly, *August 25, 1866. Courtesy of Special Collections, LSU Libraries, Baton Rouge.*

"Platform in Mechanics' Institute after the riot."
From Harper's Weekly, *August 25, 1866. Courtesy of Special Collections, LSU Libraries, Baton Rouge.*

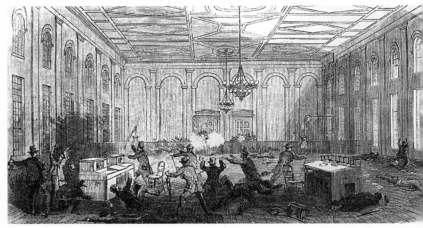

"Interior of Mechanics' Institute during the riot."
From Harper's Weekly, *August 25, 1866. Courtesy of Special Collections, LSU Libraries, Baton Rouge.*

"Carrying off the dead and wounded—inhuman conduct of the police."
From Harper's Weekly, *August 25, 1866. Courtesy of Special Collections, LSU Libraries, Baton Rouge.*

8

You Better Stay Home

JOHN MURRAL arrived for work before daylight on Monday morning at the main police station across from Lafayette Square. He was a porter, the man who laid fires, cleaned out the offices, and carried messages from the chief of police to wherever they were needed.[1] The job was a good one, especially for a black man in a city where so many black men were out of work.

This morning Murral was surprised to find the night shift still at the station instead of out on their beats. Some of the men were outside sitting in the dark on the banquette, others lounged on the gallery above the street, but most were in the cap room where the sergeant called roll. They were dressed in their usual dark blue blouses with metallic buttons and blue pants of a lighter hue, standard U.S. Army issue. But these men were definitely not in the Union army. Several sported belts they had worn while in the Confederate service, the letters "C.S." still prominently displayed on the buckles. What really set these men apart from Yankee soldiers, however, was their hats—white, straw Panamas with black ribbons for hat bands. Each ribbon was stamped in front with the officer's badge number. Murral noticed that today many of the men

1. *HSCR*, 211–12.

had turned the ribbons inside out so that their badge numbers would not show.[2]

Murral asked one of the officers in the cap room what they were doing in the station house instead of out on their beats. "We were called in," the policeman said. "We've been here since twelve o'clock last night." "Why?" Murral asked. "The convention is going to meet today, and they expect there will be a riot," he replied. "What kind of riot?" the black man pursued, but the officer evaded the question. "There may be a fuss, and we've come here by order of the Mayor to attend to the Convention."

Murral went about his duties sweeping the offices and bringing in fresh water. At eight o'clock the day shift came in. Most of them were heavily armed. Those who lacked arms were given pistols on loan from a local gun store. Murral had never seen the police so heavily armed and decided that he should warn his wife. But before he could leave, one of the men on the day shift cornered him, asking, "Are you going to the convention today?" "No," Murral said. "You better stay home," another policeman interjected. "You might get hurt." "I am not going to the convention," Murral insisted, "I have no business there."[3]

Murral left the station just after nine o'clock and went directly home. "Don't you go out today," he told his wife as soon as he got there. "Why?" she asked. "The policemen said we must keep very close. They've got pistols, bowie-knives, and clubs," he replied. "You'd better keep close." Murral then hurried back to the station before he was missed.[4]

A similar scene was being played out at the precinct houses in the city. Thomas Harris, who worked as a porter in the First District substation on the corner of Pecanier and Tapsico Streets, reported for work at half past four o'clock. The station commander, Sergeant Lucien Adams, came in shortly afterward. As usual, he was dressed all in white. Lucien Adams always wore white; the only indication that he was a policeman was a badge on his chest.[5]

2. *HSCR*, 91, 94, 167, 335; *MCR*, 127, 181. The New Orleans police force was first authorized to wear blue frock coats in 1855 but was not outfitted because of the expense (Rousey, *Policing the Southern City*, 100). In 1866, police officers were required to purchase their own uniforms, which made surplus Union army attire an attractive choice (*New Orleans Times*, August 25, 1866).

3. *HSCR*, 94, 142, 212, 286.

4. *HSCR*, 212.

5. *MCR*, 224, 259. Lucien Adams continued the practice of wearing snow-white linen suits until his death (*New Orleans Daily Picayune*, March 2, 1900).

At half-past seven, Adams called roll. Fifty-four men were present, each armed with at least one pistol. Harris helped them load. "What are you going to use these for?" he asked as he rammed a cartridge home with the loading lever. "We're going to shoot all the damned yankees," one of the officers replied. In fact, another officer told him that there was a hit list—Hahn, Dostie, Henderson, and others Harris could not remember. "I'm damned sorry for the niggers," Adams added, "but, by God, we have orders to shoot them too."[6]

The morning passed slowly for the police who lounged on the grass in Lafayette Square. All of the men from the First District main station were there, plus others who had been reassigned that morning from the Tremé station in the Second District. They were more than a hundred of them, most armed with one revolver and some with two.[7]

J. D. O'Connell, a former state senator in the Free State legislature, passed Lafayette Square on his way to the Mechanics' Institute and stopped to inquire why the policemen were so heavily armed. The New Orleans police were not supposed to carry weapons other than their nightsticks while on duty. "We mean business," one officer told him with a laugh. "Does that mean you plan to break up the convention?" O'Connell asked. "I won't say," came the reply, "but by and by we will likely have some fun." O'Connell continued on his way, disturbed by what he had seen and heard.[8]

A smaller contingent of thirty policemen assembled at the Tremé police station, laughing and adjusting their belts with one or two Colt's navy revolvers stuck in each. A few lacked pistols but carried either a knife or club instead. "What are you going to do with these things?" a citizen stopped to ask. "Never you mind," a policeman told him and sent the man on his way.[9]

It was going to be a hot day. By ten o'clock the temperature had already reached ninety degrees. The least exertion quickly brought on a sweat. The policemen at the Fourth District station on Rousseau near Jackson Street checked their weapons and perspired. One of them left and brought back four

---

6. *HSCR*, 201–3.

7. *HSCR*, 94, 109, 384, 461; *MCR*, 133, 209–10, 279. T. M. Bentley, a dentist who testified before the military commission, estimated the number of police in Lafayette Square to be from 200 to 250. He admitted that he did not count them, and his estimate seems a bit high. Richard L. Shelley, a correspondent for the *New York Tribune*, estimated that there were between 150 and 200 (*HSCR*, 476). One of General Baird's staff officers met the men from Lafayette Square as they passed down Carondolet and estimated their strength to be near 100.

8. *HSCR*, 79.

9. *HSCR*, 36; *MCR*, 70, 157.

bottles of whiskey. The men passed the bottles, interspersing swigs of whiskey with sips of ice water.[10] Whiskey with ice water did not lower the temperature, but at least it made the heat more tolerable.

Octave Breaux, the black creole who had overheard two men plotting on the other side of his fence early Friday morning, became apprehensive as time for the convention to reconvene drew near. As far as he knew, the army had ignored his warning; all Breaux could do now was confide his fears to his friends. At ten o'clock he went to the office of Thomas J. Durant. Breaux was sure that Durant would know what to do.[11]

Durant spoke to Breaux in French because that was the language Breaux was most comfortable with. Breaux repeated the story of what he had heard Friday morning. Durant was sympathetic but could not help; he had washed his hands of the whole affair.[12]

Breaux was not alone in his fears. Convention members, supporters of universal male suffrage, spectators, and curious onlookers had been warned to stay clear. "There will be bloody work," a music teacher on Camp Street told a dentist whose office was next door. "Do not go," he warned. Blacks walking up Canal became the target of taunts from white rowdies loitering along the banquette. "There goes another devil walking to his funeral," they jeered.[13]

Convention members were the target of special threats. "If I could get my hands on Cutler, that God damned negro-worshiping son of a bitch, I'll put an end to him," a policeman was overheard to say. Some of the convention members had received anonymous threats by mail. Pieces of paper four inches wide carrying the identical message were delivered to the post office and addressed to each man by name. "Beware!" the message read. "Ten Days. Duly notified. BEGONE!" The messages were signed with some cabalistic characters, below which was a rough representation of a pistol, a bowie knife, and a dagger. To strengthen the import of the communication, each envelope contained a bit of floss hemp.[14]

Many of the convention delegates had friends or associates who knew how

10. *HSCR*, 91, 168, 343–44; *MCR*, 275–76. Weather data from the *New Orleans Bee*, July 31, 1866. An afternoon rain shower in New Orleans this time of year will usually drop the temperature ten degrees, but it did not rain that day.
11. *HSCR*, 8. Durant's office was located at 18 Carondolet.
12. *HSCR*, 8.
13. *HSCR*, 17, 188, 200, 334, 361, 374; *MCR*, 50, 53, 132; "The New Orleans Horror," *Chicago Tribune*, August 8, 1866.
14. *MCR*, 140; *HSCR*, 5, 35, 361.

dangerous the situation would be and warned them to stay away. J. Randall Terry, Banks's registrar of voters and delegate to the constitutional convention, chose to stay home after his clerk, who had been in the Confederate army, told him that everybody who went to the convention on Monday would be slaughtered. Several other convention members chose to do the same—F. M. Crozat, John P. Montamat, Patrick K. O'Connor.[15]

Charles Gibbons, a veteran of the Native Guards, overheard two policemen in a corner grocery talking about plans to hang both Dr. Dostie and Michael Hahn. Gibbons set out to warn the doctor of the danger. First, he went to Dostie's house at 244 Camp Street. Dostie was not in, but Gibbons left a note telling him of what he had heard. A bit later, Gibbons went back and found the doctor at home. Gibbons repeated his warning, but Dostie was unconvinced. "I am going unarmed," he told Gibbons. In fact, Dostie had already given his revolver to his barber for safe keeping. "I know they want to take my life," Dostie acknowledged, "but I think it is a good cause to die in." Having given his warning, Gibbons left. He was on his way to join a procession of black army veterans who were going to march to the Institute to demonstrate their support for the meeting.[16]

Governor Wells sat in his office on the ground floor of the Mechanics' Institute attending to paperwork. Although Wells had been back in the city since Friday afternoon, he had not bothered to notify either Monroe, Voorhies, or Baird.[17]

The governor was working at his desk when John Burke, the former chief of police under Hugh Kennedy, came in. Burke was worried. He had seen a large number of white men in the streets near the institute that morning. He was also concerned by the large crowd of black supporters who had assembled in front of the building. Burke warned Wells that there might be a riot if the white men confronted the black crowd. "No, I do not apprehend trouble," Wells assured him. The meeting today was only to determine how many vacancies had occurred because of death or resignation so that Wells could issue a writ for the election of new delegates. In addition, Cutler had assured the governor that the delegates planned to surrender peaceably should the local authorities come to arrest them. The meeting would last for half an hour to an hour at the most, hardly enough time for anything serious to take place.[18]

15. *HSCR*, 12, 279, 325, 361; *MCR*, 55.
16. *HSCR*, 38, 124–25.
17. *HSCR*, 438. Wells had arrived at his office around nine o'clock that morning.
18. *New Orleans Daily Picayune*, July 2, 1865; *New Orleans Daily True Delta*, July 3, 1865; *HSCR*, 438, 496; *MCR*, 165.

Michael Hahn arrived at the governor's office shortly before eleven o'clock, just after Burke left. Wells showed him a telegram he had received from President Johnson on Saturday. "I have been advised that you have issued a proclamation convening the convention elected in 1864," it read. "Please inform me under and by what authority this has been done," Johnson demanded, "and by what authority this convention can assume to represent the whole people of the State of Louisiana?" Clearly, supporters of the convention could not expect any help from the president. This reality did not seem to concern Hahn, who went upstairs to the main hall. Wells also left his office to attend to some personal matters. As he left the building he saw the large crowd of blacks in front of the institute and recalled Burke's warning. Although the size of the crowd concerned him, the governor went about his errands.[19]

Several convention supporters—Howell, Cutler, Alfred Shaw, W. R. Fish, and about twenty others—met in Judge Durell's courtroom in the Custom House Monday morning to draw up contingency plans should they be arrested. Colonel A. P. Field, an experienced attorney sympathetic to their cause, was there to advise them. Together, they decided that they would not resist should the police try to arrest them. They were not armed, and Field would apply for their release on bail once they were placed in jail.[20]

After completing these arrangements, the caucus left Durell's office and walked up Canal Street toward Dryades. Along the way they encountered hostile whites, who uttered oaths and some threats, but that was all. A physician walking behind the group was surprised that they were not assaulted on the street.[21]

As they approached the institute, Howell was alarmed to find that a large crowd of black supporters had gathered, filling Dryades in front of the building and spilling toward Common and Canal. The crowd was composed of black men, women, and children dressed in their Sunday best. For them, this was a special occasion, a time to celebrate, and their eager anticipation

19. *HSCR*, 339, 438; *MCR*, 159, 166. The telegram is in *MCR* (p. 4). Wells left the institute around eleven o'clock (*GJR*, 8). Wells's testimony is inconsistent regarding his actions on Monday morning, which makes it difficult to determine his intent or the reasons he left his office. Later that afternoon, when he heard that a riot had broken out, Wells hopped on a streetcar and went to his home in Jefferson Parish, effectively distancing himself from the situation at a time when his presence was most needed.

20. *GJR*, 5; *HSCR*, 12, 18, 80, 408; *MCR*, 189.

21. *HSCR*, 12, 29; *MCR*, 177, 189.

showed. Like Wells, Howell was concerned that the large gathering would provide an excuse for the police to break up the meeting.[22]

Howell went inside the institute to the governor's office. Wells had just left, but his secretary, M. C. Sneethan, was still there. "What are they doing here?" Howell asked Sneethan, referring to the crowd on Dryades. "I suppose they came because of the speakers on Friday night," Sneethan replied. Howell went back outside and tried to get the crowd to disperse. Unsuccessful in the attempt, Howell realized that he needed someone with closer ties to the black community to persuade them to go home. The man he chose was the Reverend Jotham Warren Horton, the forty-year-old pastor of the Baptist church on Coliseum Place. Horton was from Boston, the son of a clergyman who had imprinted his abolitionist views on his son. During the war, Horton had gone south as soon as the Union army had captured the sea islands off the South Carolina coast. One of the many antislavery missionaries from Boston and New York to travel there—Gideon's Band they were called—Horton was noted for his religious zeal and insistence that the former slaves be baptized according to the doctrines of his Baptist faith. That insistence had caused some dissension among the Unitarians, and Horton had packed up and sailed for New Orleans to continue his evangelical work there.[23]

Horton went into the street and asked the crowd to leave. "Gentlemen, go home quietly," he begged. "You are not needed here. You will only create more trouble by remaining here. Please go home." Horton then asked several men in the crowd to convince their friends to leave. They tried, and some of the crowd began walking off toward Canal. Another group headed toward Common, but in twenty minutes they were back with twice the number.[24]

By this time Dostie had arrived, and he came out of the institute to talk with the crowd. Dostie liked the idea of their being there. "Good morning[,] Mr. Hughes," he said to one of the black men in the street. "Good morning, Doctor," Hughes replied. "From the appearance of things, we shall have some trouble today," Hughes noted. "I don't apprehend any," Dostie answered. "From the first indication or alarm of riot the military will be on the ground." Hughes doubted that the army could respond in time and urged Dostie to tell the men in the crowd to go home and arm themselves. Dostie demurred. "I

22. *GJR*, 6; *MCR*, 159, 177–78, 252; *New Orleans Daily Crescent*, August 1, 1866.

23. *GJR*, 4; *HSCR*, 339; *MCR*, 159, 252; Willie Lee Rose, *Rehearsal for Reconstruction: The Port Royal Experiment* (Indianapolis: Bobbs-Merrill, 1964), 180.

24. *GJR*, 5–6, 11; *MCR*, 120, 194, 264. It is likely that the women and children in the crowd took this opportunity to leave the scene. There is no record of either women or children being among the dead, wounded, or imprisoned.

don't apprehend any trouble at all," he repeated, and then he invited those who desired to come upstairs and witness the convention.[25]

Dostie was not as nonchalant as he appeared. Before he went back upstairs into the hall, he called about twenty black men together inside the vestibule. Five or six of them were armed with revolvers. Together, this group would guard the entrance to the Mechanics' Institute while the convention was in session. "Gentlemen," Dostie told them in French, "I depend on you to keep peace. Do not commence [firing] first—let them begin, [but if they do,]" he continued, "kill without pity."[26]

As time neared for the convention to reconvene, Lieutenant Governor Albert Voorhies hastened to General Baird's headquarters. In his hand he held President Johnson's reply to his telegram of Saturday. "The military will be expected to sustain, and not to obstruct or interfere with, the proceedings of the court," it read. Those instructions settled the matter of the army interfering with Voorhies's plan to arrest the convention delegates, but the lieutenant governor was still worried about a general outbreak of violence among the blacks.[27]

Voorhies showed Johnson's telegram to Baird. Baird had already seen it; a copy had been published in the morning papers. Voorhies asked whether troops would be at the institute to keep order. Baird told Voorhies that he had wired Secretary of War Stanton for instructions on Saturday evening but had not received a reply. He would not depart from his earlier plan to hold the troops in readiness until he heard from Stanton.[28]

Voorhies asked Baird to send for the troops now, but Baird vacillated. He had already rejected a request from members of the convention to protect the meeting because he did not want to be accused of favoring one side over the other. "What if both sides asked for troops," Voorhies inquired. "That would change the question materially," Baird responded. "Well, send troops to keep order and quiet," Voorhies insisted. "If a small body of troops appeared on the steps with the police," he argued, "there would be no danger of a riot being commenced on either side." Baird liked Voorhies's suggestion and agreed to

25. *HSCR*, 103.

26. *GJR*, 5, 7, 9. "Messieurs, je compte sur vous pour garder la paix, ne commencez pas les premiers, laissez les commencer, et tuez tous sans misericorde."

27. *GJR*, 12; *HSCR*, 237, 464; *MCR*, 289; Johnson to A. Voorhies (telegram), 5:40 P.M., July 28, 1866, in *MCR*, 4.

28. *HSCR*, 237, 443; *MCR*, 268, 275. Johnson's telegram was reprinted in the *New Orleans Times*, July 30, 1866.

post a few soldiers on either side of the institute as added security against a disturbance of the peace. He also promised to order a few companies to stand by in a side street, ready to respond at a minute's notice should they be called for. Voorhies set off toward the mayor's office to tell him the good news.[29]

As soon as Voorhies left his office, Baird dispatched a messenger with orders to move several companies from the 1st United States Infantry at Jackson Barracks by steamer to the foot of Canal Street. It was just past eleven o'clock.[30]

Baird was under the impression that the convention was to reconvene at six o'clock that evening, not twelve noon. The difference of six hours was crucial, for there was no way for the messenger to reach Jackson Barracks three miles downriver and have the troops embark, steam upriver against the current, disembark, and march almost a mile to the institute in less than an hour. Voorhies should have known, but because he said nothing about it during the meeting, Baird assumed that he still had plenty of time to position his men before the convention assembled later that afternoon.[31]

Having ordered the troops to the city as promised, Baird called for his carriage to find Judge Howell and inform the convention's president pro tem of the change in plans. Baird arrived at the judge's house at No. 8 Euterpe Street near Coliseum Place just as the Howells' clock struck twelve noon. Eliza Howell, the judge's wife, was upstairs and sent down word by a servant that the judge was not in. Baird asked the servant to ask Mrs. Howell where her husband was. Mrs. Howell came to the head of the stairs. "It's just twelve now, general," she said, "and he must be at the convention." "I thought that the convention was to meet at six o'clock," Baird replied. "No," she said, "Judge Howell has already gone." Alarmed, Baird got in his carriage and returned to his headquarters. As soon as he arrived, Baird ordered his aide, Captain Louis Caziarc, to go to the institute to see what was happening. He dispatched a

---

29. *GJR*, 12; *HSCR*, 237.

30. A new horse-drawn streetcar line from Jackson Barracks to Esplanade had been completed in May (*New Orleans Daily Crescent*, May 15, 1866). The limited capacity of the cars may have prevented Baird from using it as an alternative method for transporting the 1st Infantry from Jackson Barracks to the city.

31. *HSCR*, 445, 452–53; *MCR*, 274. The military board of investigation exonerated Baird for having made this crucial error. "On the morning of the riot General Baird is under the impression, shared by members of the commission and known by them to have been prevalent, that the hour of meeting was to be six p.m." (*MCR*, 38). The board of investigation failed to address the question why such an impression could have been prevalent given that Howell's proclamation of July 7, which was printed and widely distributed, clearly set "12 o'clock m" as the time for the convention to reconvene.

second messenger to Jackson Barracks to hurry the troops along, and this time he ordered a battery of light artillery to join them. The artillery would move overland.[32]

Caziarc and the courier had just left when Martin Voorhies arrived with an urgent message from his brother, the lieutenant governor, informing Baird of rumors that a black procession was forming in the Third District to march to the institute. The note also advised Baird that blacks were congregating in front of the institute and that whites had also begun to assemble at both ends of the block. Voorhies wanted Baird to station troops throughout the city to act in concert with the police. "The appearance of soldiers with policemen at this moment," he contended, "would be very beneficial." Baird assured Martin Voorhies that he had given orders for the troops to be brought up from Jackson Barracks. Given the time that had passed since his first dispatch, Baird estimated that it would take no more than half or perhaps three-quarters of an hour for them to reach Canal Street. Martin Voorhies repeated the need for troops as soon as possible. Baird reassured him that he was expecting his men at any minute.[33]

32. *HSCR*, 328–29, 445; *MCR*, 274. Baird's order read as follows: "Immediately proceed to this city with your battery, halting at the foot of Canal Street and reporting your arrival to these headquarters. Brevt. Col. Maloney has already been ordered to the city with a portion of the Infantry and will come by water transportation." (1st Lt. Nathaniel Burbank to Col. M.[?] Graham, July 30, 1866, Letters Sent, Department of the Gulf, RG 393, pt. 1, NA).

33. *HSCR*, 237, 290; *MCR*, 269, 274. The free black community in New Orleans was concentrated in the Third District, which was located downriver from the French Quarter (Anthony, "Negro Creole Community," 140).

9

Go Away, You Black Son of a Bitch

OST of the delegates who planned to attend the convention were in the main hall of the Mechanics' Institute by twelve noon. The hall was a large room 80 feet wide and 130 feet long and flanked on either side by tall windows that reached almost to the ceiling. Two large doors that opened outward onto the landing provided an entrance at one end. At the opposite end was a raised platform, in front of which was a low rail that divided the room into two unequal parts. Business was conducted inside the rail; spectators stood or sat in the larger area outside. Today, several plain chairs had been placed inside the rail in a semicircle facing the platform. The delegates sat on these chairs. On the platform there were three tables arranged in the shape of a horseshoe. Judge Rufus K. Howell, president of the convention, sat behind the table in the center. At the table to his right sat the convention secretary and his assistants. Journalists, both local and visiting, sat at a long, narrow table on Howell's left.[1]

Two to three hundred spectators had gathered outside the rail. Some had knives or pistols. A few had clubs, others carried sword canes, but most had

1. Jean-Charles Houzeau to Auguste Houzeau, August 5, 1866, in Houzeau, *My Passage*, 156.

come unarmed. Among them was a spy sent there by Judge Abell to obtain a list of convention delegates who attended. The mood was festive, but the threat of danger was in the air.[2]

About ten minutes after twelve, Howell called the convention to order. The meeting began with an invocation by the Reverend Horton, who offered a prayer for peace, the oppressed, and the Union. When Horton finished, Howell called the roll. Twenty-five of the original delegates to the convention answered. The governor's son Thomas M. Wells and another convention member arrived minutes later, making a total of twenty-seven members who dared attend. Whether for reasons of personal conviction or political convenience, they tended to the radical end of the spectrum on matters involving race. Almost all had voted for emancipation; two-thirds had voted in favor of limited black suffrage two years before.[3]

As expected, there were not enough delegates to form a quorum, nor could Howell determine which seats had been vacated. Cutler moved that the sergeant at arms round up delegates who were in the city but unwilling to attend. The motion was seconded. One of the members offered an amendment to provide the sergeant at arms with assistance so that he could execute the order more efficiently. The motion was adopted as amended, and Howell called a recess for one hour. It was twelve-thirty.[4]

A large crowd of white men had gathered less than half a block from the Mechanics' Institute at the corner of Canal and Dryades. They were joined by a large number of young boys looking for some fun. A few policemen were on duty there but not enough to control things should they get out of hand. The day was exceedingly hot, "as hot as any day [that] summer," a physician recalled. By noon the mercury had risen to ninety-two degrees.[5]

2. *GJR*, 3; *HSCR*, 403.

3. *DCCL*, 224, 450; *GJR*, 17; *MCR*, 144, 160; Charles W. Pierce, *Jotham Warren Horton: In Memoriam* (Boston[?]: N.p., 1892[?]), 11. Members of the convention in attendance were Robert W. Bennie, Terrence Cook, R. King Cutler, John L. Davies, James Duane, James Ennis, William R. Fish, J. H. Flagg, Edmund Flood, Edward Hart, John Henderson, William H. Hire, Rufus K. Howell, George Howes, H. Mass, Louis P. Normand, Patrick K. O'Connor, Benjamin H. Orr, John Payne, Eudaldo J. Pintado, O. H. Poynot, Charles Smith, John A. Spellicy, Cyrus W. Stauffer, and H. W. Waters (*New Orleans Times*, July 31, 1866). Twenty-four of the twenty-seven had voted for emancipation. Vandal argues persuasively that a majority of the delegates who came to support black suffrage did so in hopes of gaining political office or lucrative positions in the state government ("New Orleans Riot," 51, 172, 247).

4. *GJR*, 17; *HSCR*, 23, 87; *MCR*, 160, 188; R. K. Howell to N. P. Banks, August 2, 1866, Banks Collection. Seventy-six members were needed for a quorum.

5. *HSCR*, 164, 353. Temperature from the *New Orleans Bee*, July 31, 1866.

In the meantime, a procession of black men that had formed in the Third District marched through the French Quarter on their way to the institute to show their support for black male suffrage. The nucleus of the procession was made up of Union army veterans, former members of Louisiana's Native Guards. They had seen action under fire—at Port Hudson, Mansura, and Fort Blakely. Unafraid of a fight, they were armed with pistols, broomsticks, and weighted canes. A few carried slug shots. At their head were three drummers, someone playing a fife, and a man with a tattered American flag. Some said that it was the battle standard of the 1st Regiment of the Native Guards.[6]

The procession marched down Dauphine to Conti, where it turned right for one block to Burgundy and then left toward Canal. It gained recruits along the way, black men who left their work to join the demonstration. One had a carpenter's saw, another a cotton hook. The procession grew until it filled the street. Its members were determined, unafraid, and vocal, but they conducted themselves with orderly restraint. On they marched, a compact group of seventy to a hundred men headed toward an inevitable collision with the volatile throng on Canal.[7]

About the time Howell called the meeting to order, the head of the procession reached the intersection of Canal and Dryades. Three young white men standing on the banquette jeered the flag bearer. The black man waved his flag defiantly in response. Two of the men leaped from the banquette and attempted to seize the colors. Several blacks in the procession responded, and the two whites went down, crawling back on their hands and knees.[8]

At the rear of the procession, a group of white men traded insults with the black marchers. A white boy of twelve or thirteen who worked on a city streetcar shoved one of the marchers to the pavement with an oath: "Go away, you black son of a bitch." Whites on the banquette urged the boy on. The black marcher got up and hit the boy. J. A. Elmore, a Confederate veteran and now a special officer for the City Railroad Company, intervened. Pulling back the lapel of his coat to display a badge, Elmore told the black man to stop. "God damn police officer," the marcher swore as he turned toward Elmore. Elmore pulled his revolver. "I'll shoot the first man that strikes me," he warned. At that instant, someone hit Elmore with a heavy stick on the right side of the face. Legs numb, Elmore felt pins and needles. Instinctively, he fired his pistol

6. *GJR*, 5; *HSCR*, 77, 125; *MCR*, 44, 49, 112, 188, 232, 264; John Gibbons to N. P. Banks, July 30, 1866, Banks Collection.

7. *GJR*, 3, 10, 13; *HSCR*, 125, 289; *MCR*, 126, 141, 156. Estimates of the size of the procession ranged from 50 to 150 men.

8. *GJR*, 3; *MCR*, 142–43, 231.

and missed. Edward Crevon, an aide to Chief Adams, was on the scene and saw who had hit the detective. Crevon dragged the assailant out of the procession and hurried him down Canal Street toward the lockup.[9]

Suddenly, someone fired a shot at the procession from a coffeehouse on the corner of Burgundy and Canal. Several members of the procession returned the fire, six shots or more, scattering people in every direction. The three drummers beat the "long roll," just as they had during the war to rally the troops on the field of battle. "Fall in boys," they cried, "rally, boys." The procession pushed across Canal and down Dryades.[10] The two groups exchanged insults as the last of the marchers cleared the crowd, but for the time being the potential for an explosive outburst was held in check.

Judge Howell and several other members of the convention were downstairs in the governor's office waiting for the resumption of business when Baird's aide, Lieutenant Caziarc, arrived. Caziarc told Howell that Baird was under the impression that the convention was to reconvene at six o'clock that evening but had learned that it was already in session. Howell confirmed that the convention had already reconvened but told Caziarc that it was in recess until one-thirty. Howell also told Caziarc that he did not intend for the convention to sit later than three. When Caziarc asked what the convention members planned to do if the civil authorities decided to intervene, Howell assured him that they would submit to arrest without resistance. Satisfied with what he had learned, Caziarc set out for Baird's headquarters.[11]

Just as Caziarc left the building, the procession arrived in front of the institute. Supporters of the convention greeted the procession excitedly. The black veterans gave three cheers, and the crowd cheered in return. The flag bearer stood on the steps of the institute, waving his banner defiantly at the whites on Canal.[12]

Several marchers went inside and up the stairs to the hall, taking the flag with them. Most members of the procession stayed in the street, however, and mingled with the crowd sitting on the banquette. Chief Adams, who had been

9. *GJR*, 4–5, 11–12; *HSCR*, 188, 204, 401; *MCR*, 112, 255–56, 264; *New Orleans Times*, July 31, 1866.

10. *GJR*, 4, 6, 8, 11–12; *MCR*, 44–45, 49, 121, 188, 196; John Gibbons to N. P. Banks, July 30, 1866, Banks Collection. Several witnesses claimed that the first shot came from the procession, but the preponderance of testimony suggests that the first shot was fired at rather than by the procession (e.g., *GJR*, 12).

11. Howell (*HSCR*, 47), Caziarc (*HSCR*, 464–65).

12. *GJR*, 4; *HSCR*, 72, 104; *MCR*, 182, 196, 250.

at the Common Street end of Dryades when the procession arrived, walked past them on his way toward Canal. "All those people up the street are rebels and should be cleaned out," a black man in front of the institute challenged as the chief walked by. Adams let the comment pass, not wanting to provoke a confrontation. Fortunately, the situation remained calm, and Adams decided to return to his office.[13]

The atmosphere among supporters of the convention continued to be festive. Some of the men were drinking, and a few of them began to show the effects of alcohol. Concerned that the celebrating was getting out of hand, someone inside the institute sent a black man into the street to ask the crowd to disperse. This was not a public meeting, the man told them; go away and be quiet. But they would not go and cheered even louder. Another black man, older than the first, also addressed the crowd, asking it to break up. He, too, was unsuccessful.[14]

Shortly before one o'clock, the trouble started again. The white boy who had tangled with the procession when it crossed Canal Street ventured up Dryades and began taunting the black crowd. "Damned sons of bitches!" he yelled. Several black men with sticks advanced toward him. The boy retreated toward Canal until he came to a pile of bricks in the street, building material for a house under construction. There he made a stand, a brick in each hand, and dared the men to touch him. One of the police officers on duty at the corner of Canal and Dryades rushed up from behind and grabbed the boy by the collar. "Stay back," the officer warned. "Take him away and kill him," yelled one of the blacks as the officer dragged the boy down the street. "No, no; let him go," shouted the crowd of whites on Canal. Several black men followed as far as the pile of bricks and began throwing them at whites on the corner. Then it happened: one of the black men pulled out a revolver and fired.[15]

The whites on Canal rushed up the street toward the institute. The black men behind the pile of bricks retaliated with shots of their own. The two sides clashed briefly, and the whites fell back, firing their pistols in return. Two black men were left lying on the pavement, one dead and the other dying. A third lay close by, badly injured. Several whites wounded during the skirmish were carried off by their friends.[16]

---

13. *GJR*, 13; *HSCR*, 77; *MCR*, 144.

14. *GJR*, 4, 10; *MCR*, 116, 195, 250, 254, 282. The correspondent for the *New Orleans Times* reported that one of the two speakers was attempting to incite the crowd to riot (July 31, 1866).

15. *GJR*, 4, 7, 10, 17; *HSCR*, 77, 251–53, 334; *MCR*, 116, 120, 193, 216, 221, 251, 255, 264; *New Orleans Times*, July 31, 1866; John Gibbons to N. P. Banks, July 30, 1866, Banks Collection. For the time the riot started, see *MCR*, 119, 158, 268, and *HSCR*, 55.

16. *GJR*, 4; *MCR*, 96, 143, 179.

The white mob rallied in Canal Street. Many of the men were armed with revolvers; the boys carried bricks, clubs, and stones. A young man held a bloody slug shot with black hair stuck to it. "What is that?" Rush Plumly, a former superintendent of education for the Freedmen's Bureau, asked the young man. "I have just killed a nigger with that," he boasted.[17]

Some of the police and a few citizens attempted to restore order. Charles Beyer, a second lieutenant in the 81st Infantry, was in Ricketson's confectionery when he heard the firing. Someone in the store wondered aloud whether something could be done to prevent bloodshed. Beyer said he would try. Running out into the street, he accosted a policeman and asked him to help. "You go to hell," the officer replied. Refusing to give up, Beyer placed himself in front of the whites on Canal Street and tried to keep them back. Several policemen joined him in the attempt. One man with a brick in each hand refused to obey. Beyer knocked the bricks out of his hands, and the man pulled a knife out of his boot. "You Yankee son of a bitch," he sneered as he made a sweeping cut at Beyer. A policeman came to Beyer's aid and smashed the man across the head with his nightstick. For a few minutes, the commotion died down. Someone suggested bringing up one or two fire engines to drench the crowd with water, but no one paid attention.[18]

Chief Adams was sitting in his office when a young clerk came running through the door. "It has started," he blurted. "The negroes are shooting at people on the sidewalk." Adams decided that it was time to order his men to the Mechanics' Institute. The fire alarm operator knew what to do. From his desk he sent out the twelve-tap signal. It was one o'clock.[19]

The police in Lafayette Square formed into ranks and started up St.

17. *HSCR*, 353; *MCR*, 143.
18. *GJR*, 5, 8, 10, 15; *MCR*, 44, 173, 217, 282.
19. *GJR*, 13; *HSCR*, 309. It is difficult to determine from the testimony, some of it conflicting, at what time the twelve-tap signal sounded. It does seem definite that fighting had broken out before the alarm, despite the testimony of one witness who asserted that he heard the signal before the procession reached Canal (*HSCR*, 327). A dentist, Dr. T. M. Bentley (*MCR*, 133), passed Lafayette Square at ten minutes before one o'clock and saw the police still assembled there. By the time he got to Common Street, they had started their response, which would place the twelve-tap alarm at just a few minutes before one o'clock. This observation would correspond to policeman Oscar Marcour's testimony (*MCR*, 240). Also see testimony from Dalzell (*MCR*, 48) and Brooks (*MCR*, 51), whose estimates varied from a quarter before to a quarter after one o'clock. The *New Orleans Times* (August 1, 1866) placed the ringing of the alarm bell at ten minutes past one o'clock.

Charles as soon as they heard the alarm bell strike twelve times. They turned left at Poydras and then right on Carondolet. "There goes Hays's brigade," a civilian standing on the banquette said as the police passed. From Carondolet they went up Common until they reached Baronne, where a detachment split off to cover the rear of the institute. The remainder continued up Common toward Dryades.[20]

The twelve-tap alarm also sounded in all of the twenty-three firehouses throughout the city. Several companies, including Columbia No. 5 on Girod near City Hall, started for the institute to assist the police. They were armed with revolvers.[21] Although they realized that the signal was not for them, they also knew what it meant. Things had gotten out of hand, and the police might need their help.

When Lucien Adams heard the alarm bell, he called for his men to assemble outside the First District substation on the corner of Pecanier and Terpsichore. "I want you to make yourselves very active," he told them as they filed out the door. "Make yourselves lively; see what you can do." They were almost two miles from the institute and would have to hustle to get there in time.[22]

The fifty-four men fell into line on the banquette. They were veterans of many battles and certainly not afraid of a fight. They started off at a trot with Adams and his two corporals in the lead. The band turned right on Camp and continued until they came to Lafayette Square as the first prisoners were coming in. Some of Adams's men wanted to tear into them. Adams motioned them off; there was more important work to do.[23]

Police from the Second District converged on the institute from two stations, one at Tremé market and the other in the arsenal behind the Cabildo on Jackson Square. "Gentlemen," Lieutenant William H. Manning told his men when he heard the alarm, "I want you all to do your duty." At the Tremé station a corporal went into the yard at the sound of the twelve taps and asked for ten volunteers. Ten men stepped forward and followed the corporal up Dauphine to Canal. The two detachments of police from the Second District reached the intersection of Canal and Dryades about ten minutes after the alarm sounded. "Boys, keep quiet and cool," Lieutenant Manning ordered, "no one move before I give you orders." One of the blacks in the street near

20. *MCR*, 109–10, 138.
21. *HSCR*, 136, 180, 213.
22. *HSCR*, 203.
23. *HSCR*, 70, 213.

the institute fired a shot at the crowd. "Clear the street," Manning ordered. Twenty policemen advanced in a skirmish line, just as they had done during the war. About fifty white civilians tagged along behind.[24]

A black man stood at the pile of bricks as Manning's men advanced. When the police were almost on him, he took off down the street. Several black men hid in doorways along Dryades and fired at the police as they swept up the street. The police returned fire as these men raced from one doorway to the next. Thomas Cooney, who had once served as General Banks's bodyguard, jumped up on the pile of bricks. "Come on," he urged the police, "don't stand back and be cowards." Some blacks rushed inside the institute, but others continued up Dryades across Common to escape.[25]

Martha Waters had the misfortune of owning a boardinghouse on the other side of the vacant lot next to the institute toward Canal. One of the black men in the street ran into the elderly black woman's yard. "You can't come in here," she yelled. "I'll have no fuss in my yard." Mrs. Waters pushed the young man out and locked the gate. But the pile of bricks was just beyond her gate, and several blacks hid behind it in the street next to her fence. When the police moved in, several of the men jumped the fence into her yard. The police followed in hot pursuit, breaking the gate and pushing down the fence. Some of the black men ran into Mrs. Waters's house. The police followed, cornering the fugitives, shooting and beating them wherever they were found.[26]

One of the fugitives was shot trying to escape through Mrs. Waters's backyard. Slowed by his wound, the man was an easy target for an ax-wielding police officer who overtook him. "You black son of a bitch," the policeman grunted as he struck the wounded man square in the head. Jefferson Johnson, a boarder, was watching with his wife through the curtains from the second floor. They were scared to death. Before long there was a pounding on the door to their room. "Who's in there," a voice demanded. "Nobody but my

24. *GJR*, 5–6; *HSCR*, 40; *MCR*, 152, 157, 169, 196, 207. Manning was a former major in the 6th Louisiana Infantry who had seen action as part of Hays's Brigade in the Army of Northern Virginia. Although born in New York, Manning had fought for his adopted state, being wounded in 1862, captured in 1864, and paroled to serve with his regiment until surrendering at Appomattox (Booth, *Records of Louisiana Confederate Soldiers*, 2:864; *OR*, 36: pt. 1, 1023, 36: pt. 2, 148, 46: pt. 1, 1271, 42: pt. 3, 1195). The *New Orleans Bee* commented on the "military precision" with which the police swept the street (July 31, 1866). Henry Clay Warmoth entered a similar observation in his diary entry for July 30, 1866 (Warmoth Papers).
25. *GJR*, 6, 9; *MCR*, 121, 148, 154, 156, 196, 214, 222, 251.
26. *GJR*, 5; *MCR*, 219, 222, 235, 237; also *New Orleans Times*, July 31, 1866.

husband," Johnson's wife replied. "Let me see," the man demanded. She opened the door, and a civilian stepped through. Spying Johnson, he fired a small pistol loaded with bird shot, striking Johnson in the forehead. Just then, a policeman came into the room. "Let him go," he said, "I'll take him in charge." The officer escorted Johnson into the front yard, where another policeman came up and hit the black man across the face with a loaded cane before taking him to jail.[27]

Inside the boardinghouse, the policemen broke open trunks and slashed mattresses looking for weapons. In a doorway to one of the boarder's rooms, an officer confronted Ann White, one of Mrs. Waters's maids. Putting a pistol to her breast, the excited policeman threatened with misdirected enthusiasm to "blow her brains out." "Master, don't shoot me," White cried. "You're one of the damned convention," he accused. "I don't know anything about it," she pleaded. Fortunately for White, another policeman intervened and told the other man not to trouble her. "She's a poor woman," he told his comrade. But while this exchange was going on, a policeman downstairs broke into Ann White's trunk and stole a silk dress worth $23. Throughout the house, money, clothes, cutlery, and anything else of value was taken away. Thomas Burns, an officer from the First District, left his hat band behind, a black ribbon with No. 168 printed in front. When he was asked about it later, Burns claimed that he could not remember his badge number.[28]

Out in the street Manning's men caught up with a few blacks here and there. One police officer prodded a tall black man with a full beard by hitting him repeatedly over the head with the butt of his revolver. The black man did not strike back but shielded his head and face with his hands, protesting each blow. Satisfied that he had taught the man a lesson, the officer then turned his attention to two black men hurrying toward Common on the opposite side of the street. One of the men was Charles Gibbons, the former captain in the Native Guards who had tried to warn Dostie that morning. The policeman recognized him. "There goes one damned nigger captain, the son of a bitch," he cried. "Kill him." Gibbons and his comrade, a veteran of the same regiment, began to run. "Let's turn around, and we may have a chance to dodge the balls," Gibbons yelled to his companion. They had used this trick during the war. He had gone about ten steps backward when his friend let out a groan and put his hand to his side. "I am shot," the friend cried; "I am killed." Gibbons turned and ran as fast as he could. He made it as far as the corner of

27. *MCR*, 219–20, 237.
28. *MCR*, 219, 235, 237.

Common and Baronne before he ran into the police from Lafayette Square on their way to the institute. The street was now sealed, and blacks who had not made it across Common before the police arrived were trapped inside the institute.[29]

Dryades itself was empty, except for three black bodies. The police kept the large crowd of whites back on Canal. For the moment, order had been restored. The police spread out, surrounding the institute, and prepared to deal with the convention itself. Two delegates to the convention, Cyrus W. Stauffer and James Duane, watched from the entrance of the building as the police took up their positions. "Jim," Stauffer remarked, "they look as if they are going to come for us."[30]

29. *HSCR*, 125; *MCR*, 81, 193. Gibbons was arrested and taken to jail. One witness, Evans (*HSCR*, 197), testified that the police from both districts arrived at the two ends of the block simultaneously. Although they did arrive at about the same time, other testimony indicates that the police on the Canal end of Dryades had started their sweep before police from the First District arrived at the corner of Common and Dryades.

30. *GJR*, 15; *HSCR*, 18; *MCR*, 226–27, 237, 239. Stauffer was a convention delegate who had led the floor fight that stripped Abell's antisuffrage provision for blacks from the emancipation article to the constitution.

10

For God's Sake, Don't Shoot Us!

S PECTATORS and members of the convention inside the institute did not know what to expect. W. L. Randall went to the window and looked out on Dryades. He could see a wounded black man lying on the banquette across the way, but otherwise the street was clear. As he stood there, a policeman in the street below spotted Randall and took a shot. The bullet struck the sash and shattered the glass about two feet above Randall's head.[1]

The shot excited the spectators in the hall. Some began to pray; others began singing hymns. "What shall we do?" someone cried; "we have no means of defense." Six or seven of the spectators in the hall were armed. One of them took out his revolver and positioned himself by a window. "Put that down," another told him, "you may shoot me!"[2]

Cutler and some of the others were concerned that the presence of the black spectators would give the police a reason to attack the hall. Cutler asked them to go home; they were not wanted here. There would be trouble if they stayed. Reluctantly, some of the crowd began to file out of the hall, down the

1. *MCR*, 141.
2. *HSCR*, 160, 254; *MCR*, 132, 141, 148, 180, 224.

stairs to the vestibule below, and out into the street. The police had sealed off both ends of Dryades and blocked the alleyways leading to Baronne. The crowd halted, not knowing what to do.[3]

They did not have to wait long to decide. The police and a large number of white civilians began to advance from both ends of Dryades toward the institute, firing as they came. It sounded like a "pack of fire-crackers you put on the banquette," one of the policemen recounted later. Sometimes their target was a face in the window of the hall; mostly it was someone in the street.[4]

The black men in Dryades broke into two groups and began fighting almost back to back against the white advance. Slowly, they gave ground until they were forced to withdraw into the vestibule that fronted the institute. They continued to resist, some with revolvers but mostly with bricks and stones. A large black man stood in the entrance, his face and hands covered with blood, holding a large rock over his head to defend himself. The wounded lay in the vestibule, their blood drenching the tiles under the columns.[5]

Upstairs in the hall, R. King Cutler stood on the platform and called on everyone who was not armed to congregate inside the rail, the portion of the hall furthest from the entrance. He directed those with firearms to stay outside, near the door. Only a handful of men, perhaps a dozen, remained outside the rail. "Gentlemen, all of you sit down," Cutler told the crowd. "We are peaceably assembled here; do not move." The crowd was slow to respond. "Do as you are told," Dostie yelled, "if you have not chairs sit down on the floor, EVERYBODY!" The Reverend Horton moved through the assembly as they crowded behind the rail. "Sit down, sit down," he told them, "place your trust in God." Some sat on chairs, others on the floor. Turning to William P. Judd, the sergeant at arms, Cutler directed him to close the windows and not let anyone go near. The large double doors leading into the hall were left open as evidence that the convention did not intend to resist.[6]

Five minutes after the men in the hall had settled anxiously into chairs or

3. *MCR*, 145, 229.
4. *MCR*, 169.
5. Houzeau, *My Passage*, 129–30.
6. *HSCR*, 35, 65, 339, 498; *MCR*, 118, 138–39, 145, 180, 187. There is some disagreement in the testimony as to whether the doors were left open. Although they were most certainly closed and barricaded after the first rush by the police into the hall, it appears that they were left open initially in keeping with the conventioneers' intention not to resist arrest. John Gibbons's account of the riot in his letter to Banks (July 30, 1866, Banks Collection) suggests that the doors were closed after the police occupied the landing.

crouched on the floor, three policemen appeared in the doorway, pistols drawn. Behind them were seven more on the landing. Without a word, the three officers opened fire. "For God's sake, don't shoot us," voices in the hall cried out; "we've done no harm; don't shoot us; we are peaceable." A black spectator attempted to grab one of the doors to close it, but an officer on the landing aimed his pistol at the man through the crack between the door frame and the door. The black man let go and ran back into the crowd. "For God's sake," Cutler cried out, "do not fire any more." The policemen continued shooting. Dostie was on the stage when a ball hit him in the arm. "I am shot," he exclaimed. The officers retreated to reload after they had emptied all the chambers of their revolvers. Several black spectators ran to the doors, closed them, and began to pile chairs in front of the entrance. Dostie tried to reassure the crowd. "Be patient, be patient," he told them, "the military will be here in a few moments."[7]

The doors into the hall opened outward, which made it difficult to bar entry. Nevertheless, a black man took hold of a doorknob and pulled with all his might. Randall saw that the man could not hold both doors closed and told him to let go. The man did as he was told and rushed behind the rail. The doors swung open. J. D. O'Connell went forward with both hands outstretched, a white handkerchief in one, to talk with the officer in charge. "I implore you men to cease firing," he called out. "These people do not wish to fight, and have nothing to fight with." He told the officer that everyone in the hall was prepared to surrender if the police would protect them. O'Connell and the policeman shook hands, and O'Connell helped him clear some of the chairs that were blocking the door. The police came in and formed a line across one end of the hall. "Now, boys, we have got them," the officer yelled, "give it to them!" They opened fire a second time.[8]

This time the police advanced further into the hall, emptying their revolvers as they came. One officer succeeded in getting almost to the rail before a black man got behind him with a heavy stick and hammered him down. A few of the spectators returned fire. Supporters of the convention were beginning to fight back. Using broken chairs, they rushed the police and drove them out. The police beat a hasty retreat, stumbling down the stairs to the vestibule. Several members of the convention followed the police onto the landing, crying, "Don't shoot!"[9]

7. *HSCR*, 65, 120, 158, 339, 401; *MCR*, 118, 138, 180, 187. The police claimed later that they had been fired on first (e.g., *MCR*, 153–56), but physical evidence and the number of casualties led the military commission to discount their testimony (*MCR*, 42).
8. *HSCR*, 36; *MCR*, 141, 229.
9. *HSCR*, 36, 87, 158; *MCR*, 49, 118, 120, 138, 145, 229.

The appeals for a cease-fire were to no avail. Outside, the police had climbed into the upper floors of the Medical College and the gallery of Mrs. Waters's boardinghouse on opposite sides of the institute, where they could fire directly into the hall from both vantage points. Their shots shattered the windowpanes, showering those crouching on the floor with shards of glass. Occasionally, someone was hit. Gustave Chevalier saw a black man at one window receive a ball in the throat. Many of the shots went high and passed completely through the hall, whistling as they flew. Unfortunately, these shots gave the police on the opposite side of the building the impression that the people inside the Mechanics' Institute were shooting back. Accordingly, they redoubled their fire. Most of the people in the hall huddled on the floor, hoping that the army would arrive in time to stop the bloodshed.[10]

While the police regrouped downstairs for another assault, a white spectator in the hall ran to the United States flag by the platform, tied a white handkerchief to the tip of the staff, and stuck it out a window. His effort to signal surrender was greeted with gunshots from the street. Some of the spectators had gone to the windows and had begun to shoot back when the policemen on the landing forced the doors open a third time and rushed into the hall.[11]

This time, the Reverend Horton stepped forward with a white handkerchief tied to a small staff from one of the flags. Other people, lying on the floor and cowering behind the rail, took out handkerchiefs and pieces of white cloth to indicate their desire to surrender. "We surrender, we are peaceable," Horton said. "Don't fire, take us prisoners, but don't fire." A policeman raised his revolver and fired twice, hitting Horton in the arm. Horton fell to the floor but struggled to his feet. Some of the spectators returned fire, and a policeman standing at the door fell. The rest retreated, taking their wounded comrade with them. Rebuffed in their attempts to surrender, those who remained in the hall realized that they had to escape if they were going to survive.[12]

There were four ways out of the hall. The obvious exit was down the stairs that led from the landing to the vestibule on the ground floor, but the police were there, and anyone taking this route would also have to get past the mob in the street. Nevertheless, J. D. O'Connell escaped by this route. Seeing the police retreat down the stairs to reload, O'Connell leaped over the stair banis-

10. *HSCR*, 35, 78, 197, 295, 385; *MCR*, 159, 180, 187, 219; Houzeau, *My Passage*, 129.
11. *HSCR*, 333; *MCR*, 118, 151.
12. *HSCR*, 12, 36, 78, 158, 339; *MCR*, 141, 154, 207.

ter just as they started back up. Surprised, the police tumbled back down the stairs and out into the street, where O'Connell slipped away in the confusion.[13]

Another way out of the hall was to dart from the landing up the stairs to the offices on the fourth floor, where a person might be able to hide until the carnage was over. Several members of the convention, including Cutler, made their way to the fourth floor while the police were regrouping in the vestibule for another assault.[14]

A third escape route was down the stairs on the outside of the building at the rear of the institute. The door to these stairs opened from a small room on the left side of the platform. William P. Judd, the convention sergeant at arms, unlocked the door leading to the room, and a dozen people, including Judge Howell, crowded into the small space. In his excitement, Judd could not unlock the outside door to the stairs. Howell opened a window and started to step out onto the stairs. "Judge, stay in, stay in; you will be killed," one of the party implored. "I must go out," Howell replied, "I must go to the governor and get him to send for the military." Howell climbed out onto the stairs that descended into the courtyard bordered on one side by a low wall that separated the institute from a furniture maker's shop facing Baronne. The rest followed. Some reached Baronne through the furniture shop and made good their escape. Others followed Judge Howell to the governor's secretary's office on the ground floor.[15]

Thomas Wells, the governor's son, was in the secretary's office and let the small party in through a side door. Howell sat down at the secretary's desk in the outer office to write an urgent plea to General Baird to send troops. He had written only half a line when the police surrounding the building fired another volley, aiming their shots for the hall above. Several stray balls passed through the windows below, showering the men crouched inside with broken glass. Howell tumbled behind the desk and hid until the younger Wells suggested that they retreat to the governor's office, where they would be safer. Once there, Judd made Howell sit in the fireplace and draped an American flag around him. Judd instructed the others to sit with their backs against the brick wall. Several times police or members of the mob tried to open the door but, finding it locked, went away.[16]

Barring use of the stairs at either end of the building, the only other way

13. *HSCR*, 79, 339, 493; *MCR*, 181.
14. *HSCR*, 373; *MCR*, 123.
15. *MCR*, 130, 146, 160, 164; Houzeau, *My Passage*, 157–58.
16. *MCR*, 146, 160–61, 164.

to get out of the hall was to jump through the windows. The distance from the windowsills in the hall to the ground was more than twenty feet. E. E. Sinclair leaped from an east window and hit the ground. Jumping up, he dashed to a fence behind the building and started to clamber over when he came face to face with a policeman on the other side. "Where did you come from, you damned son of a bitch," the startled officer demanded as he stuck his cocked revolver into Sinclair's face. "From the building," Sinclair answered. "I'll shoot you," the policeman snarled. "What do you want to shoot me for," Sinclair entreated, "I have done nothing." "You damned Yankee son of a bitch," the officer cried as he grabbed Sinclair and marched him off to the police station, his revolver still aimed at Sinclair's head.[17]

The west side of the institute bordered the backyard of the Medical College. Beneath the rearmost window of the hall was an outhouse for the college. A. Delage, a former officer in the Union army and reporter for the *Springfield Republican*, jumped from the window onto the roof of the outhouse and slid down into the school yard below. Delage had a white handkerchief in his hand and attempted to surrender to a policeman who accosted him. "I was merely a spectator," Delage insisted. Unimpressed, the officer struck Delage with his nightstick. "I would far sooner you should fire on me, if you are not a coward, that you should break my head with a club," Delage challenged. The policeman paid no attention. "In five minutes another damned rascal's gone," he muttered. Fortunately for Delage, Chief Adams came up at that moment and demanded, "Who assaulted this man?" "Negroes," the officer told Adams, although there was not a black man to be seen in the yard. Adams detailed two men to take Delage to the doctor's office and ordered them to put their charge in a cab after his wounds were dressed and take him home.[18]

Others were not so lucky. Two black men who jumped into the yard of the Medical College were set upon by police and citizens and killed. But a few white spectators escaped by jumping onto the roof of the outhouse and then making their way through the back of the furniture maker's shop on Baronne. "Gentlemen there is no road for you here," the owner told them as they passed through. "I presume we can go through," one of them challenged as he pulled off his coat. "We will pass through as workmen," which they did, blending into the crowd and slipping away undetected. The same was not true for a black man who chose the same route. The store owner called for the police,

17. *HSCR*, 76, 103, 118, 155, 295; *MCR*, 145.
18. *MCR*, 138, 159.

who arrested him and took him outside. Later, the store owner found the man lying on the banquette in front of the store, dead.[19]

The supporters of the convention who still remained in the hall were growing desperate. O. H. Poynot went to Dostie. "The military has not come," Poynot said, "we must get out of here." "Poynot," Dostie told him, "if you go out with me you are bound to be murdered; go out alone, and you have a chance." The two men shook hands. "Doctor, I must go out," Poynot said. "I expect to be killed," Dostie replied, "all I regret is that I have nothing to defend myself with."[20]

By this time, men had formed two rows on the landing, one on each side of the door and down the stairs to the vestibule. These were not policemen but members of the mob acting in concert with the police. Convention delegates and spectators had to pass through this gauntlet to reach the street.[21]

Poynot waited for a pause in the firing and made a break for the door. Two policemen reloading their pistols stepped out to stop him. "Gentlemen, I am at your mercy," Poynot exclaimed, "I am your prisoner; I surrender." "That's Poynot, a member of the convention," one of the two exclaimed, "we must kill him anyway." The officer swung at Poynot with a loaded cane. Poynot warded off the blow with his arm. He caught a second blow with his hand. The second policeman hit Poynot in the head with his nightstick. Another policeman grabbed Poynot by the collar and dragged him to the head of the stairs, where someone hit Poynot behind the ear with his fist. Poynot fell down the stairs and rolled to the bottom. "Kill him," several of the crowd in the vestibule cried. Fortunately, Police Lieutenant Joseph Jacobs from the Third District was there and knew the prisoner. "Gentlemen," Jacobs replied, "I am in charge. I will shoot down the first man that injures him." Jacobs got Poynot out of the building and turned him over to a police officer who took the dazed delegate to jail.[22]

The police began beating John Henderson on the stairs as they escorted him out of the building. Holding his hand over his head and begging for his life, Henderson went down as soon as he stepped onto the banquette. The crowd closed in crying, "Kill him, kill him; he's one of the negro worshippers." Somehow, Henderson got to his feet and ran along the plank fence toward

19. *HSCR*, 118–19; *MCR*, 135, 150, 171, 207, 213; also *New Orleans Times*, July 31, 1866.
20. *MCR*, 199.
21. *HSCR*, 88; *MCR*, 50, 201, 229.
22. *MCR*, 199–200, 241. The police officer's name was John Marcner.

Common. Before he got to the end of the fence, he fell, and the crowd closed in again. The beating continued for several minutes until up went a great hurrah. "They have killed the God damned nigger son of a bitch," someone shouted.[23]

W. R. Fish, Sr., was more fortunate. After Horton was shot, Fish went out onto the landing, where Sergeant Edward Thomas placed him under arrest with the promise that he would protect him. Thomas called for four of his men to assist him, and they led Fish down the stairs into the street. Dryades was packed with people. A cry went up when they saw Fish. "Hang the damned Yankee," they yelled, "hang the white nigger!" A man jumped up on a lamppost and tied a rope to the top in order to carry out the threat. Thomas and his men led Fish to Canal and turned toward the river on the way to the Second District station at Jackson Square. The crowd was still dense, and several of the mob attempted to hit Fish with bricks and sticks. One of the crowd got close enough to hit Fish in the head with a club. Fortunately, it was a glancing blow. Thomas and his men kept the mob back and turned Fish over to Lieutenant Charles Ramel from the First District on the corner of Canal and Camp. Ramel commandeered a cab, placed two officers in it to protect the prisoner, and ordered the driver to take Fish to the precinct station.[24]

When Michael Hahn came out, the crowd went wild. "There's old Hahn!" they cried, "kill him! hang him!" Two policemen held him on each side. Hahn had a club foot, and his long crutch stuck out in front. When they reached the edge of the banquette, someone fired a shot. Hahn drew himself up to his full height, as if to challenge the would-be assassin. Then someone threw a brick, which struck Hahn on the back of the head, and his feet went out from under him. The crowd closed in; the policemen called for Chief Adams, who was on the other side of the street. Adams helped push the crowd back, knocking down several citizens in the process. The crowd closed in again, and the police protecting Hahn had to beat them back. The police retrieved Hahn's crutch and carried him along toward Common. Adams commandeered a carriage on Carondolet and started back to Dryades. "My life is in danger," Hahn cried out to Adams as he turned to go. "I insist upon your going with me." Adams assented and climbed aboard with one of his officers. Even then the crowd

23. *HSCR*, 199; *MCR*, 139.

24. *HSCR*, 12, 41, 477; *MCR*, 81, 110, 124, 172, 282; *New York Times*, August 1, 1866. Ramel fought in the western theater as a Confederate private until his capture at Vicksburg. After being paroled, Ramel was promoted to corporal and served until the Confederate army surrendered at Meridian, Mississippi, on May 13, 1865 (Booth, *Roster of Louisiana Confederate Soldiers*, 3:241).

closed in, and the policeman pulled out his revolver and dared anyone to interfere. "The man is dying," he cried. "Leave him alone." The carriage started off down the street with Adams and his colleague guarding their prisoner all the way to the lockup.[25]

Constance Loup, an assistant sergeant at arms for the convention, who had been born in Neuchatel, Switzerland, was not so lucky. The thirty-five-year-old clerk was temperamental but popular. He had joined the 1st New Orleans Infantry when it was organized in April 1864 and had been commissioned a captain because of his well-known Unionist views. But Loup had difficulty getting along with his fellow officers and seemed to favor the bottle more than the responsibilities of the command. At one point, another officer preferred charges against Loup. Absent without leave, drunk and disorderly, and "conduct unbecoming an officer and a gentleman" were among the ten allegations brought to the attention of his superiors. Loup disputed the absent without leave charge, claiming that rheumatism of the foot had left him incapable of carrying out his duties. But apparently Loup could still get around, for "carousing around the city of New Orleans" was one of the charges of which he was accused. Somehow, Loup survived the court-martial and was honorably discharged on June 1, 1866, just weeks before the convention.[26]

When Loup reached the street, the mob recognized him instantly. "Charge the god damned yankee nigger worshipping son of a bitch, kill him," they cried. Loup broke free and ran to his left down Dryades toward Common. The police fired several rounds at the moving target, while the crowd threw bricks at his head. Policeman Earhart ran after him with a big knife in his hand. "Here goes a god damned yankee son of a bitch," he yelled as he overtook Loup just as he reached the Medical College. Earhart plunged the knife into Loup's side and turned to walk back to the institute as the mob closed in on the hapless Captain Loup. Armed primarily with clubs and bricks, they began pounding the prostrate body. Satisfied that they had done the work, several men cheered, "We have fought for four years these god damned yankees and sons of bitches in the field, and now we will fight them in the city."[27]

Alfred Shaw, a convention supporter who had been sheriff of Orleans Parish before Hays's election, received similar treatment. As Shaw and his captor made their way through the mob on Baronne Street between Common and

25. *GJR*, 7, 11; *HSCR*, 172–73, 199, 286, 293, 354; *MCR*, 56, 114, 140, 220, 258. Later that night, Hahn sought out Chief Adams and thanked him for saving his life (*HSCR*, 286).

26. Loup's Compiled Military Service Record, NA.

27. *HSCR*, 154, 199; *MCR*, 140. Fox testified that Earhart stabbed Loup in the back, but the surgeon's report indicated that the knife penetrated the abdomen.

Gravier, a civilian rushed up behind him and shot him in the back. Shaw took off his coat and saw blood coming from a wound in his shoulder. "Well, that's a damned shame to shoot a man in the back when in the hands of the police," one of the crowd remarked. "It ought to have been put behind his ear," someone quipped.[28]

Dostie's appearance sent the crowd into a frenzy. "There's Dostie," they yelled, "kill him! kill him!" The police escorted Dostie up Dryades toward Canal. They had gone only a short distance when the mob closed in. The police released Dostie and backed away. A small boy picked up a brick and threw it at Dostie, and several of the crowd moved in with their revolvers drawn. "You assassins," Dostie muttered as a man in shirt sleeves and white pants fired. Dostie staggered, and the policemen again took his arms. "Protect me, protect me," he implored. A man in a gray linen coat behind Dostie fired a shot into the doctor's back. The ball severed his spinal column. Dostie fell forward on his face. Using his arms, he rolled over on his back and put his hands over his eyes. Still, the mob would not let him be. A group of men with white handkerchiefs tied around their necks grabbed Dostie by his legs and started dragging him down Dryades. The doctor's head bounced on the pavement. When they reached Canal, the men stopped in front of a cake shop and gave a cheer for Jeff Davis.[29]

28. *MCR*, 234.
29. *GJR*, 13; Jourdain (*HSCR*, 205); *HSCR*, 119; *MCR*, 108, 124, 143–44, 147, 236, 245–46.

11

Hurrah for Hell

I N DRYADES the scene was wild. The shrill sound of police whistles filled the air, and there was much yelling. "Hurrah for hell!" a drunken rowdy waving a pistol yelled, "Hurrah for Louisiana!" Another man stood in the street, with clenched fists and tears in his eyes. "It's a shame! It's a shame," was all he could say.[1]

There was an absolute crush of people at both ends of Dryades at Common and Canal. These were mostly civilians. In front of the institute there was a smaller but more aggressive force made up mostly of police but with civilians mixed in. Together, they outnumbered the members of the convention and spectators five to one.[2]

The police had lost control. Men were running everywhere. Vagrant boys joined in the fun. They had been too young to fight in the war; now it was their turn to do battle. They hurrahed, laughed, and shouted. "Now they are going to get it!" they cried with glee.[3]

Dr. James B. Cooper was on his way to visit a patient when he passed the

1. *GJR*, 15, 17; *HSCR*, 16; Report from the *Cincinnati Commercial* reprinted in *The New Orleans Riot: "My Policy" in Louisiana* (Washington, D.C.: Daily Morning Chronicle, 1866), 7.
2. *MCR*, 178.
3. *GJR*, 7; *MCR*, 134, 220, 261; entry for July 30, 1866, Warmoth Diary, Warmoth Papers. Vandal's demographic analysis of the mob indicates that it included a cross section of white New

intersection of Canal and Dryades after the mob rushed the institute. First, he saw two men shot down in the street. Then two blacks ran past him followed by whites armed with clubs. One of the black men was elderly. Dr. Cooper recognized one of the pursuers as a one-armed former Confederate soldier. "Kill the damn niggers," the man yelled, "kill them!" The mob caught up with the two men near the neutral ground. Their clubs did their work; both men were beaten to death.[4]

At the corner of Dryades and Common a fire engine plunged through the crowd on its way to the institute. The driver was obviously drunk. Several on-lookers yelled, "They're going to fire the Institute!" Even if the rumor had been true, this fire engine would not have been any help, for there was no fire in the box and no steam to drive the pump. But it did have something the police wanted—pistols. The engine stopped in front of the institute, where firemen opened the side box and started handing out revolvers. Firemen helped the police on Canal Street as well. They brought up three boxes of cartridges so that the policemen could reload after they had exhausted their ammunition.[5]

As the riot progressed, the mob was strengthened by the arrival of unemployed whites and low-life types who were naturally attracted to trouble. Many of these men were drunk. A large man of about thirty on a brown horse with crutches tied to the saddle rode among them, urging them on. Each time a member of the convention was brought out, he would yell, "Kill those damned convention sons of bitches." A Confederate veteran who had lost both arms during the war shouldered his way through the crowd urging them on. "Kill all the damned sons of bitches in the building," he yelled, "don't let any escape."[6]

As the mob swelled and the fury of the riot escalated, many rushed into local gun stores to purchase arms. Although Griswold and Company on the corner of Canal and Royal closed its doors as soon as the shooting started, a large crowd shoved and pushed their way into Hyde and Goodrich's. There were so many customers that they spilled out into the street. Dart and Watkinson also did a brisk business. Watkinson closed the doors and had his black porter put up the shutters so he could let the customers in a few at a time. On several occasions policemen came into the store for more ammunition. Wat-

Orleanians. It was not composed only of "lower class citizens," as at least one historian of Reconstruction has asserted ("New Orleans Riot," 250–53).

4. *HSCR*, 140.

5. *HSCR*, 83, 157, 328; *MCR*, 202; also *Cincinnati Commercial* in *New Orleans Riot*, 7.

6. *HSCR*, 281, 461; *MCR*, 135, 238, 286; *New Orleans Times*, July 31, 1866. As an ironic twist, the armless veteran was later appointed to the post of sergeant at arms at the statehouse.

kinson gave it to them at no charge and had his porter load their revolvers for them in the store. A large number of citizens also bought revolvers and loaded their guns before going back out on the street. Watkinson did a brisk business all day, although he refused to sell a gun to a drunk who was shot through the leg and shoulder. That night when he finally closed, he had taken in $1,198 for pistols and ammunition. It had been a banner day.[7]

"Have you shot anybody today?" Lucien Adams asked Bill Balestier, a young member of the mob, as the police sergeant rallied his men at the corner of Common and Dryades. "No," Balestier said, but he showed Adams his revolver. "Come with me," Adams ordered as he led the young man through the crowd. Adams went about his business with the calm of a professional killer. While taking a drink in Gary Owen's coffeehouse on Common Street between Dryades and Rampart, Adams saw a black man across the street walking past the gate at No. 233. Without a word, Adams rushed out of the coffeehouse and shot the man dead. The victim's sister came to collect the body later that afternoon.[8]

The police had plenty of help. In addition to the uniformed officers, there were twenty to thirty police trainees in civilian dress who could be identified by metal badges, a crescent around a star, pinned to their coats. Hays's special deputies were in civilian dress too but wore a blue ribbon in the buttonhole of their lapels for identification. There were also several firemen, some in uniform and some in civilian dress, helping the police. The firemen wore white handkerchiefs around their necks so that they would not be confused with the convention delegates they were trying to arrest. Veterans of the Washington Artillery could be identified by the crests they wore on their lapels—crossed cannon on a red field encircled by a wreath. Others in the crowd were easy to identify because they were wearing their old Confederate uniforms.[9]

Supporters of the convention coming out of the institute had no choice other than to make a run for it. When one appeared, the mob would "run for him like dogs after rats coming out from a wharf," as one observer put it. The mob fired indiscriminately as the blacks emerged. "Here come those black sons of bitches," one cried as he opened fire. A black man attempted to beat

7. *HSCR*, 187; *MCR*, 55, 191–92, 210–12, 238, 240, 255, 272, 286.
8. *HSCR*, 193; *MCR*, 221, 247.
9. *HSCR*, 2, 14, 80, 94, 99, 110, 125, 186, 195, 208, 340; *MCR*, 115, 144, 151, 182, 228, 233, 243, 245. Chief Adams testified that he had stationed the trainees on St. Charles Street to keep them away from the institute, but apparently they rushed to the scene of action and joined in the affray as soon as the riot began.

his way through the crowd with the back of a chair. He made it as far as Common before he went down with several pistol balls in his body. The scenario was repeated over and over. Whites at both ends of Dryades intercepted blacks who made it through the mob in front of the institute. First, they would shoot until the man was brought down. Then the mob would close in and pound the victim with bricks and clubs until he was dead.[10]

Sometimes a delegate got lucky and recognized someone he knew among the police or in the crowd. Recognition often meant protection, and he was taken to the precinct station under guard. In these instances, the police were effective in keeping the crowd back and protecting their prisoner.[11]

Chief Adams did what he could to hold the mob in check. Whenever he witnessed an assault, he arrested the assailant and sent him to the lockup. At times, Adams had to restrain one of his own officers who had lost control. On one occasion, he struck a policeman with his cane because the officer was flogging a black man. Unfortunately for the supporters of the convention, Adams could not be everywhere at the same time.[12]

The chaos spread out from the Mechanics' Institute and flowed into streets nearby. One black man had the misfortune of getting off the streetcar at the entrance to an alley beside the institute that led from Baronne to Dryades. The mob beat him with sticks and pummeled him with stones until someone came up and finished him off with a pistol. The body lay across the streetcar tracks until someone dragged it aside to the gutter.[13]

John Burke, the former chief of police under Mayor Kennedy, who had warned Governor Wells of the impending trouble earlier that morning, emerged from the backyard of the Medical School through a door in the brick wall after having slipped out of a window of the ground floor. On his way out he passed several policemen crouched behind the wall firing up toward the windows on the second floor. One of them grabbed Burke and shoved him up against the wall, knocking off his hat. Recognizing the former chief of police, he let him go. Burke stooped to pick up his hat when a brick hit the dusty ground in front of his face. Temporarily blinded, Burke stood up, only to be hit in the head by another brick. As he crumpled to the ground, Burke was shot in the side. Burke stumbled into Baronne and started toward Common. At the corner, he saw the police on Dryades and a mob on Common near St.

10. *HSCR*, 110, 180, 186; *MCR*, 120–21, 163, 233, 253.
11. *HSCR*, 70, 88; *MCR*, 122, 147, 163, 225, 288.
12. *HSCR*, 145, 286, 309; *MCR*, 114; *New Orleans Times*, July 31, 1866.
13. *MCR*, 128, 146.

Charles. Burke hastened back down Baronne to Canal, where he turned right and made his way to Dr. O. Anfoux's office on Canal Street to receive medical attention.[14]

Often the mob caught up with their quarry several blocks from the institute. Two policemen chased a black man down Baronne to Gravier. He left bloody tracks on the banquette as he ran. One of the policemen shot at the man twice, hitting him the second time. The man fell, and the policeman ran up and pulled the trigger of his revolver. It snapped; the chambers were empty. Frustrated, the policeman struck the black man three or four times with the butt of his gun. After the two policemen left, the black man raised his head and made a gurgling sound. A white man standing nearby approached. "Damn you," he exclaimed, "ain't you dead yet?" With that, the white man kicked him several times in the face and pushed the dying man into the gutter.[15]

The mob attacked many blacks who had nothing to do with the convention. Alfred Campbell, for example, was walking down Gravier on his way to meet a friend for lunch when he ran into four or five police officers coming back from the station house. Campbell did not realize that the convention was meeting at the institute a block and a half away. Nevertheless, the policemen knocked him to the pavement and fired. The ball passed between Campbell's arm and side. Campbell jumped up and ran up Gravier past Rampart to Circus (now Loyola), with the police and several citizens chasing him. Just as Campbell reached the rear of Taylor's Stables, a dry goods clerk named Andrews stepped in front of Campbell and hit him in the head with the lid of a packing box. Reeling from the blow, Campbell stumbled into the stables, where Nelson Taylor, the owner, struck him with a heavy oak armchair. Campbell fell, and Taylor kicked him in the side. A policeman ran up and fired two shots at his prostrate form before forcing him to his feet and carting him off to the lockup.[16]

An elderly black man, sixty or seventy years old, was chased down Gravier by five or six citizens with pistols in their hands. When they caught up with him, he stopped. "What is it, Massa?" he asked. One of the pursuers placed his pistol to the old man's head and blew his brains out.[17]

---

14. *HSCR*, 493; *MCR*, 149. The first initial in Dr. Anfoux's name and the location of his office are from the "Business Directory" in *Gardner's New Orleans Directory for 1866* (New Orleans: Charles Gardner, 1866), 506.

15. *HSCR*, 111; *MCR*, 137, 190, 233.

16. *HSCR*, 186; *MCR*, 176, 232. Nelson Taylor denied to the military commission that he had participated in this incident (*MCR*, 247).

17. *HSCR*, 159.

Volney Hickox, a correspondent for the *Cincinnati Commercial*, was at the telegraph office at 9 Carondolet just off of Canal Street, filing a report for his paper when the edge of the riot reached him. Hearing a commotion outside, Hickox walked to the door in time to see a black man break free from the mob at the corner of Common and Carondolet and run down the street. Citizens standing along the banquette struck at him as he passed. Finally, a white man grabbed him by the hair in front of the telegraph office and threw him into the gutter, where he jumped on the black man and started hitting him with his fist. Hickox stepped out of the office and pushed the man off. Pulling the black man inside the building, Hickox took him upstairs for safety.[18]

While Hickox was inside, another black man dressed in a dark coat and white pants broke free and ran down Carondolet toward Canal. Five policemen chased him, firing as they went. Edward Brooks, a correspondent for the *New York Tribune*, had just arrived at the telegraph office when the police caught up with him near the door. One of the policemen put his revolver to the black man's head. "Don't kill that man," Brooks ordered, "arrest him." "You nigger loving son of a bitch," the policeman snarled. "I will arrest you next," he said, and shot his prisoner through the head.[19]

Over on Canal Street, a black man ran down the neutral ground followed by half a dozen members of the mob and one policeman. Someone threw a club, which caught him on the head, and he fell. He was shot five or six times as he lay there. Just down the street, another black man came running out of Baronne and made it to the neutral ground before he too was shot dead.[20]

Two white men in shirt sleeves and armed with bricks chased another black man down Canal Street toward Bourbon. Three policemen were right behind them. The black man ran as fast as he could, but one of the white men caught up with him and knocked him down with a brick. The black man jumped up to run again, but the other white man got in front and stuck out his foot to trip him. Another brick struck his head, and two of the policemen caught up in time to finish the job with their revolvers.[21]

The police chased two young black men, no more than sixteen or seventeen, up Canal to Basin, where Frederick Brooks, a boardinghouse landlord, shot them as they ran. "Today is the white man's day," he boasted, "I will shoot everything I can get in range of."[22]

The crowd loved it. A drunken policeman put his arms around a boy as the

18. *MCR*, 97, 202.
19. *MCR*, 51, 134; see also *HSCR*, 477.
20. *MCR*, 97.
21. *MCR*, 126, 144.
22. *MCR*, 240.

young man loaded his revolver. "You're a good boy," the policeman shouted. "You know who to fight for, who your friends are." A wounded black man asked another policeman why he did not arrest some of the white rioters. "Shut up, or I'll blow your brains out," was the reply.[23]

As the frenzy continued, more and more civilians were swept away in the ebb tide of fury. Mary Ann Larkin, an Irish prostitute, chased several black men as they fled, hair flying and clothes disheveled by her pursuit. "Kill the black sons of bitches, kill the black sons of bitches," she cried. Finally, she caught up with one who had been slowed by the stroke of a club in the hands of one of the mob. The two fell together. Larkin had a broken sword cane about six or eight inches long and cut him across the face and chest and once in the arm, which stuck out stiff like a mannequin. Satisfied, Larkin jumped up and ran after some other blacks she spied down the street, although the work of death left her too breathless to catch them.[24]

Casualties, arrests, and escapes reduced the number of spectators and members of the convention in the institute to the point that the police were able to secure the building. James Duane, a member of the convention, was hiding in a closet on the ground floor as the police moved through the institute. "For God's sake, master, master, do not kill me," he heard a black man in the hall above him cry as he dropped to his knees. "I have nothing to do with this; I have no arms; I was just passing; do save my life, master." "Get down, you black son of a bitch," Duane heard policemen reply, followed by the muffled sound of shots through the floor boards.[25]

Gustave Chevalier was a spectator who crawled through a hole under the stairs to the platform when the firing became heavy. Chevalier crouched in the small space along with four others as the police cleared the hall. The killing was systematic. "Oh, this man is not dead; he is pretending," Chevalier heard from his hiding place. A pistol shot followed. When everyone in the hall was dead, the police and citizens began breaking up the room. "Damned Yankee sons of bitches," they cursed as they broke chairs and smashed furniture. Suddenly, Chevalier heard a tearing sound. There was nothing in the room to tear, he thought. Then he realized that they were tearing the United States flag. "Damned abolitionists," Chevalier heard them mutter.[26]

23. *MCR*, 127.
24. *MCR*, 232–33, 254, 267; also see John Gibbons to N. P. Banks, July 30, 1866, Banks Collection.
25. *MCR*, 227.
26. *MCR*, 187–88, 246. The shredded flag was apparently the one used by the procession. Chevalier and his companions remained under the stage until the army occupied the building, at which point they made their way home unharmed.

George Nelson climbed into a garret on the fourth floor, where he found a man with a bandaged head who was also hiding. The police finally found them and ordered the wounded man down. "What are you doing there, you God damned son of a bitch; come out of there, God damn you, come out." The man did as he was told, and when he got close enough the policeman put his pistol to his head and fired. Nelson expected the same treatment but was assaulted instead by another officer with a stout stick. The first officer joined the second in beating Nelson, shattering the arm that Nelson threw up to protect himself. Later, while Nelson was lying in the street with the other wounded, someone stole $70 from his back pocket.[27]

R. King Cutler was more fortunate. At half past three, four policemen found him wedged in a space between a joist and the roof. "There's one of them," one of the policemen cried, "look at his feet. Come down, you damned son of a bitch, come down," he ordered. Cutler let himself down. When they reached the landing on the second floor, Cutler asked to be allowed to look into the hall. He saw the smashed furniture and several dead bodies. Hats, caps, and other articles of clothing were strewn on the floor. Bullet holes scarred the walls, particularly behind the platform. There was so much blood on the landing that it squished under his feet. Two more dead men were in the vestibule downstairs. Although his captors cursed Cutler heartily, they did not harm him when they reached the street, possibly because Chief Adams was there and ordered them to protect their prisoner.[28]

Five men, two white and three black, had climbed through a skylight onto the roof of the institute, where the police found them. The police arrested the two white men and took them to the station. A citizen shot the three black men dead.[29]

With their breakup of the convention complete, the police took a breather. Many of them stretched out in the shade of the trees lining the neutral ground in the middle of Canal Street. Others went off in search of water and liquor. It was hot; the temperature stood at ninety-nine degrees by midafternoon.[30]

Judge Abell stood before the members of the grand jury. He had called them to order at twelve noon, precisely the time the convention had planned to reconvene at the Mechanics' Institute. They were there to indict the members of the convention who had shown up for the meeting.[31]

27. *MCR*, 175.
28. *GJR*, 15; *HSCR*, 29–30, 309; *MCR*, 131; *New Orleans Times*, July 31, 1866.
29. *HSCR*, 144, 252; *MCR*, 142.
30. *MCR*, 276. Temperature from the *New Orleans Daily Bee*, July 31, 1866.
31. *HSCR*, 246.

The indictments had been prepared in advance; all that was needed was to fill in the names. Thanks to his spy, Abell now had the names: Bennie, Cook, Cutler, Davies, Duane, Ennis, Fish, Flagg, Flood, Hart, Henderson, Hire, Howell, Howes, Mass, Norman, O'Connor, Orr, Payne, Pintado, Poynot, Charles Smith, Spellicy, Stauffer, and Waters.[32]

One by one, the names were entered. Sheriff Hays stood by, ready to serve the writs when they were finished. Sometime around three o'clock, the writs had been perfected. Ignoring their agreement to check with General Baird before serving the writs, Hays left Judge Abell's chambers to arrest the delegates for participating in an "unlawful assembly dangerous to the peace and good order of the State."[33]

32. It is likely that Thomas Wells was not indicted because he missed the roll call and did not show up on most lists of delegates in attendance (e.g., *GJR*, 16).
33. *GJR*, 12; *HSCR*, 246, 442–43; *MCR*, 268, 273.

12

Can I Go Home?

S URGEON GEORGE W. NEW observed the police taking prisoners
to the lockup from the steps of his office at No. 127 Carondolet just
around the corner from City Hall. Dr. New thought that some of the
police were drunk. Many of their charges were wounded, some seriously. Others seemed unharmed. The police hurried all of them down the street, striking
some of them with nightsticks because they were not walking fast enough.
One black prisoner was shot through the thigh and could not walk as fast as
his captor wanted. The officer hit him in the face with his pistol to encourage
him along. Another policeman struck his prisoner on the shoulder with a cotton hook. The Reverend Horton passed by in custody. Horton was bareheaded. "Can I go home, can I go home?" he pleaded.[1]

Two policemen escorted a wounded black man down Common toward
Carondolet. A third officer crossed the street and held his pistol six inches
from the man's head. He fired once, and the man fell to the banquette. Officer
Scully, one of Adams's "extras," guarded his prisoner until they reached Gravier. Taking a step back, Scully drew his revolver and shot the man, hitting
him in the neck. Scully left the wounded man lying where he was.[2]

1. *HSCR*, 164; *MCR*, 122, 129.
2. *HSCR*, 186; *MCR*, 200. "Extras" were supernumeraries (see Chapter 7).

An old black man wearing a private soldier's blue Union army blouse stumbled along in the custody of a policeman. He had been shot through the lungs. "Move along," an officer ordered. The old man was bleeding internally and close to collapse. The officer struck him twice hard in the face with the butt of his pistol. The old man fell and then struggled to his feet, asking for mercy. "God damn you," the policeman snarled, "you did not crow that way yesterday!"[3]

The scene was repeated in the French Quarter as police herded their prisoners to the lockup in the arsenal behind the Cabildo Square. A young woman who lived on Royal saw the police beating their prisoners as they took them to jail. In particular, she was horrified at the sight of an old black man who could hardly walk. The police hit him with their nightsticks on the head, turning his white hair red with blood.[4]

At the Tremé station the police telegrapher, P. A. Caseaux, tried to stop the beating of a black man brought in under arrest. Caseaux was a veteran of the Union army but had retained his job after Monroe's purge of the police force because of his telegraphic skills. "Gentlemen," Caseaux shouted, "you must not do that. Stop it." "He must get the same as the others," one of them replied. "He is under my protection," Caseaux told them. "If you touch him you will have to touch me!" The police did not heed his warning, so Caseaux pulled his revolver. "Gentlemen," he repeated, "if you want to hurt that man you will have to hurt me." Only then, seeing that Caseaux was serious, did they stop beating the man.[5]

Police who were not busy taking prisoners to the lockup fanned out from the institute. William Hanksworth, a civil engineer, had just taken his seat in a streetcar on Canal when a black man rushed into the car with two policemen chasing him. The policemen caught him as he reached the front platform and dragged him back through the car, striking him with their nightsticks. Hanksworth could not bear to watch and turned his head. The car continued on its way, turning down Rampart. Hanksworth looked up, only to see two policemen assault another black man on the corner of Rampart and Custom House Street (now Iberville). The man fell to his knees, and it seemed to Hanksworth that he was begging for his life. Just then the car turned the corner, and Hanksworth did not see what followed.[6]

---

3. *MCR*, 129.
4. *MCR*, 164.
5. *MCR*, 70. Caseaux was discharged from the police force two weeks after the riot.
6. *HSCR*, 178.

Charles James witnessed police officer Billy Tier board a streetcar near the Clay Statue and shoot an old black man. James watched as a young black boy on the car tried to hide behind one of the seats. Officer Tier shot him, pulled him out of the car, and threw him on the pavement. Going back into the car, Tier pulled the old man into the street, where he stood over his two prisoners, cursing them in French.[7]

On Dauphine Street, more than ten blocks from the institute, a policeman stopped Manuel Kohn, a black schoolmaster. A fireman came running up and yelled, "Here's one of those fellows!" The two officers pulled Kohn out of his buggy, hitting him with a nightstick. Kohn was bleeding about the face as the policeman marched the schoolmaster off to the lockup. Meanwhile, the fireman robbed Kohn's black coachman of his money before ordering him to drive on.[8]

Martin Self sold watermelons from the house he rented on the corner of St. Phillip and Claiborne Streets several blocks from Canal. He had been tempted to close up and go see what was happening at the institute but decided against it. Self was still in front of his house when officer Auguste Cook came by on his way back to the station with a black prisoner. Seeing Self inside the doorway, he drew his revolver and demanded, "What are you doing here?" "I live here," Self explained. Cook pulled his whistle and blew it three times. His partner, George Sykes, came running. Sykes put a pistol against Self's side and ordered him to fall in with the other prisoner. Hearing the commotion, Self's wife came to the front door and began to cry. Cook told her to shut up or he would arrest her too, and she retreated into the house.[9]

Officers Cook and Sykes marched Self and the other man down the street toward the station. "You damned niggers thought you were going to take the town, didn't you," Cook said. "I was only selling my watermelons," Self replied. "I wasn't trying to make a fuss." Cook was angry. "We are going to clean all you damned niggers out," he muttered as he stepped back and fired his revolver, hitting Self in the hip. Self fell to the pavement, and Cook fired again, but the shot only grazed the wounded man. As Cook reached into his pocket

7. *HSCR*, 189.

8. *HSCR*, 123–24.

9. *HSCR*, 337–38; *MCR*, 46, 288–89. Martin Self testified before the military commission in August and the House Select Committee in December. His testimony differs in some of the details. Although the account given here draws from both statements, the earlier one is relied on more heavily because of its proximity to the events related. Boyer's account is also closer to Self's testimony in August. Cook's and Sykes's first names are from the police roster published in the *Daily Crescent* on May 28, 1866.

for more cartridges, Self jumped up and ran. Sykes fired three shots, two of them hitting Self in the back. Remarkably, Self stayed on his feet and made it to the intersection, where he was stopped by another policeman. The incident had drawn a crowd, some of whom were sympathetic to Self's plight. "Don't you see that he is shot now," someone offered. "Let him go home." Others spoke up, telling the officer that Self had not been to the institute and that he had done nothing wrong. At that moment, Self's wife ran up, pleading for his release. The officer wrote down Martin Self's name and let him go home to his watermelons.[10]

Something had to be done about the dead bodies that littered the streets around the Mechanics' Institute. There were fifteen on Dryades between Common and Canal, five at the corner of Dryades and Canal, and another ten or twelve on the neutral ground in Canal. Nine bodies lay at the corner of Baronne and Common, six more at Common and Carondolet. Mrs. French went to her front gate at No. 220 Common Street at the intersection with Dryades to find two dead black men lying there. The heat was such that many of the bodies had begun to swell in the sun. White citizens of New Orleans, men and women, gathered to look and then walked away.[11]

The police commandeered dray wagons, two-wheeled carts, and furniture wagons to carry off the dead. Prisoners from the workhouse were used to load the gruesome cargo. The prisoners threw the bodies in the wagons like dead sheep. Arms and legs protruded over the sides. But some of the victims were still alive. Peter Crocker, a black spectator in the hall, had been shot through the right eye, the bullet exiting from the top of his head. He also had a dirk stuck in his side. Remarkably, he survived and lay on the pavement for two hours in the hot sun. At one point a white crowd gathered over his body. "God damn him I think he's not dead yet," one of them remarked. "God damn it, he is dead," another said, "don't you see all his brains are out?" "I think I saw him wink," exclaimed yet another. "Oh, God damn it, he is dead as hell," the second man retorted, "only the sun makes him wink." Finally, the police came to load Crocker onto the dead cart. One of them pulled the dirk out of his side. They threw Crocker into the wagon with his heels up and head down. They moved on down the street, throwing bodies on top of him until they reached the workhouse, where inmates began to unload the dead. Crocker got

10. *HSCR*, 337–38; *MCR*, 45, 288–89.
11. *HSCR*, 145, 154, 156; *MCR*, 45, 179, 234; "The New Orleans Horror," *Chicago Tribune*, August 8, 1866.

his heels up over the side of the cart so they could see that he was still alive. Without comment, they pulled him out and put him on the ground until they could find another wagon to take him to the Marine Hospital. The surgeon who treated Crocker believed his to be one of the most extraordinary cases he had ever seen.[12]

Unlike Crocker, Constance Loup was certainly dead. In addition to the stab wound in his side, he had three shots in his head—two in the forehead and one behind the ear. His skull was fractured and cracked open on each side behind the ears. Four more shots were in his body, although the knife had probably done its work long before these other wounds were inflicted. Even then, the mob was not satisfied. After Loup's body had been thrown in a furniture wagon for the trip to the morgue, a watch repairman named Frank picked up a brick and smashed the dead man in the face.[13]

Four policemen picked up A. P. Dostie's body lying in the neutral ground on Canal Street and shoved it halfway into a small, two-wheeled cart. Incredibly, Dostie was still alive. One of the policemen climbed over the side and pulled Dostie all the way in. Two other policemen got on top, and as they drove away, one of them took off Dostie's hat and waved it in the air. A crowd of more than a hundred who witnessed the event cheered and followed the cart up Canal Street.[14]

Mayor Monroe showed up at Baird's headquarters shortly after two o'clock. "When will the troops arrive?" he demanded. Baird told him that he expected them at the foot of Canal Street any minute and was just on his way to meet them. "Will they be white troops?" Monroe inquired. "A portion of them will be white, and a portion of them colored troops," Baird replied. "Will they act along with the police?" Monroe asked. "I will suppress the riot," was all that Baird would say in response to Monroe's last question.[15]

A few minutes later, Captain Caziarc returned and told Baird that a riot was going on around the Mechanics' Institute. J. D. O'Connell, who had gotten out of the building by jumping over the banister on the landing, also reached Baird's headquarters and told him of the situation. "For God's sake," O'Connell implored, "send the military!" Baird told him that he would, as

12. *HSCR*, 111, 343, 477; *MCR*, 234, 242–43. The *New Orleans Times* reported on August 1 that three live men were found among the dead.

13. *HSCR*, 365; *MCR*, 228. The knife penetrated Loup's large intestine and liver, causing internal hemorrhage (*New Orleans Times*, August 1, 1866).

14. *MCR*, 97, 126, 199.

15. *HSCR*, 445; *MCR*, 274, 289.

soon as they arrived. O'Connell tried to impress on him the urgency of the situation to no avail. "I understand my business," Baird replied, adding that he could do nothing until the troops arrived.[16]

Soon after O'Connell left, Baird rode with his staff officers to the foot of Canal Street to meet the troops who were just disembarking from the steamer. It had taken them more than three hours to make the trip. Baird marched the men at a double-quick up Canal to the vicinity of the institute. A section of artillery, which had also arrived, unlimbered at the foot of the Clay Statue at the intersection of Canal and St. Charles. A black man running from a knot of pursuing whites darted between the guns to safety. Baird ordered the infantry to fan out down both sides of Canal, securing the street as they advanced. He proceeded with another detachment to the Mechanics' Institute and assumed control of the building from the police. Baird then divided his men into patrols and sent them through neighboring streets to disperse what remained of the mob. It was four o'clock.[17]

When the area around the institute was secure, Baird returned to his headquarters to dictate an order. "In consequence of the notorious and unlawful proceedings today," the order read, "martial law is proclaimed in the city of New Orleans." Baird appointed Major General A. V. Kautz military governor. Just as he finished his dictation, Sheriff Hays arrived with the writs for the arrest of the members of the convention. Finding the institute under the control of the army by the time he got there, Hays had come to Baird's headquarters to ask permission to serve the warrants. Baird did not even bother to open the document. Ordering Hays not to make the arrests, Baird took out his pencil and scrawled on the outside of the paper, "The sheriff will withhold further action on this writ until further orders."[18]

For Howell and the others hiding in the governor's office, the first indication that federal troops had arrived was the sight of two mounted men in uniform followed by a squad of infantry marching up Dryades from Canal. Still, they waited. Not until Howell saw three Union officers approaching the institute

16. *HSCR*, 79, 464.

17. *GJR*, 4; *HSCR*, 170, 309, 445; *MCR*, 275; also *Chicago Tribune*, August 8, 1866; Kenneth E. Shewmaker and Andrew K. Prinz, eds., "A Yankee in Louisiana: Selections from the Diary and Correspondence of Henry R. Gardner, 1862–1866," *Louisiana History* 5 (Summer 1964): 294.

18. *HSCR*, 446–47; "The Convention of '64," *New Orleans Bee*, July 31, 1866. Baird's proclamation was issued around six o'clock (Shewmaker and Prinz, eds., "A Yankee in Louisiana," 294).

did he leave his hiding place. But when Howell reached the vestibule, a policeman stopped him. "How did you get into the building?" the officer demanded. "I've been here all day," Howell replied. The policeman grabbed the judge and announced that Howell was his prisoner. Just then the three federal officers reached the steps. "Are you a member of the Convention?" they asked. "Yes," Howell replied. "Am I to go with this gentleman?" he asked, motioning to the policeman. "We have nothing to do with it," one of the federal officers replied, and the policeman marched Howell along the banquette, blowing his whistle as he went. A second policeman came running, and the two of them escorted Howell toward the police station on Lafayette Square, their pistols drawn. Neither man realized that they had the president pro tem of the convention in their custody. "He's a damned nigger conventioneer," they called out as they walked. Although the crowd along the route was abusive and made threatening comments, the two policemen protected their prisoner.[19]

When Howell reached the lockup behind City Hall, he found dozens of battered and wounded prisoners huddled in cells. The Reverend Jotham Horton was lying in a crowded southwest corner cell on the ground floor, barely conscious. "Take me to the Carrollton depot," he begged, "I want to go home." William Waters, a member of the convention, took off his undershirt, wet it, and tied it around Horton's head. Waters also tried to get the city physician, Dr. E. Caire, to attend to the victim, but the doctor refused. "He got just what he deserved," Caire told Waters.[20]

Howell was kept in one of the crowded cells for about twenty minutes before he was moved to a room upstairs with two other prisoners. S. E. Planchard, an army veteran of the Mexican War, was thrown into a cell full of blacks. "Go in there among your negro friends," they told him. Dostie lay on a blanket in the prison courtyard. A second blanket, folded over, served as his pillow. It was clear to everyone that he was dying.[21]

The cells became more and more crowded as new prisoners arrived. Joseph R. Piquee, a physician, was one of those arrested and thrown into a cell. Seeking to soothe the wounded, Piquee asked for wet cloths to bathe the wounds of his cellmates. They gave him water and salt instead. L. H. Panza begged for a glass of water. "Damned black Yankee republican," was the only response he received. Dr. Caire looked in occasionally but did nothing. "You got just what

19. *HSCR*, 48; *MCR*, 161.
20. *HSCR*, 37, 76, 165, 191, 357. The city physician's name was obtained from the "Municipal Record" in *Gardner's New Orleans Directory for 1867* (New Orleans: Charles Gardner, 1867), 576.
21. *HSCR*, 48; *MCR*, 82, 161, 204.

you deserved," he told the prisoners, wounded and well alike. "You joined the Yankees, and you must expect what you got."[22]

Prisoners were also locked up at the Second District station at Jackson Square. Lieutenant Colonel Schuyler Crosby arrived late that afternoon to find the pavement in the prison yard covered with dead and dying. No effort had been made to alleviate their suffering. "The whole scene was more like a slaughter-pen for animals," Crosby recalled, "than a receptacle for human beings who were to be protected by the civil authorities."[23]

At City Hall, Mayor Monroe fretted about the inability of the police to maintain order. Given the excessive heat of the day, most were exhausted. Monroe needed "extras" to supplement the force. Around five o'clock Mayor Monroe issued a proclamation.[24]

> Whereas the city is in a state of great agitation arising out of the riots precipitated by a revolutionary faction; and whereas it is absolutely necessary that order be restored and violence suppressed;
>
> Therefore, I, John T. Monroe, mayor of the city of New Orleans, do call all such citizens as are willing in maintaining the peace to appear at the City Hall this day at 6 p.m., to be sworn in as extra policemen. No one not holding my authority will be allowed to make any arrest.
>
> All good citizens, with the exception of those on duty, are requested to retire to their homes, and not to assemble in crowds on the public streets.[25]

White New Orleanians were eager to respond, and hundreds of citizens rushed to City Hall, where they were given blue ribbons to put in their buttonholes and deputized. Fearing that blacks were going to burn the city to the ground, Monroe ordered a double guard placed at each fire station and directed that the firemen carry guns when they responded to a blaze.[26]

General Kautz arrived at City Hall around nine o'clock. "Is this Mr. Monroe?" Kautz asked. "Yes, sir," Monroe replied. "I am directed, sir, to relieve you of any duties as Mayor of this city and assume command as Military Governor of New Orleans," Kautz informed him. Monroe protested. The police

22. *HSCR*, 99, 248, 357.
23. *MCR*, 120, 262.
24. *HSCR*, 218, 445–46.
25. Monroe's proclamation appears in *MCR*, 126.
26. *HSCR*, 348; *MCR*, 56, 67–68; also see *New Orleans Times*, August 1, 1866.

had put down the riot, and the army had done nothing until they showed up four hours late. Now Baird had usurped Monroe's civil authority by declaring martial law.[27]

Kautz was unimpressed. He asked what steps had been taken to move the wounded from the jail to the hospital. The mayor told Kautz that the wounded had already been moved. Crosby, who had just returned from the lockup at Jackson Square, disputed Monroe's assertion. Nothing had been done to remove the wounded prisoners or relieve their suffering.[28]

Kautz directed Crosby, Major M. V. Sheridan, and Dr. G. W. Avery to the station house across the street from City Hall to inspect the prisoners. The wounded were to be sent to two clinics, whites to Charity Hospital, blacks to the Marine Hospital, which was operated by the Freedmen's Bureau. Kautz directed Crosby to release the unwounded prisoners who were being held because of their association with the convention.[29]

The lockup at Lafayette Square consisted of twelve cells—six above and six below with three on each side of a central corridor. Each was approximately twenty feet square. Crosby opened the door to the first cell and almost vomited. The prisoners were crowded on top of each other, begging and crying for water. Many were standing on wounded men lying on the floor. With twenty or more in each cell, there were more than two hundred men in custody there.[30]

Dr. Avery immediately went to work. On more than one occasion Avery kneeled to ask a prisoner where he was hurt only to find that the man he was talking to was already dead. The temperature in the cells stood at more than one hundred degrees.[31]

Dr. Caire had been drinking and was of no assistance, although he followed Dr. Avery from one patient to the next. "Let that cuss be," Caire would insist. "Damn him, he's not hurt any." In spite of Caire's objections, Avery instructed Major Sheridan to go out into the street and commandeer carriages and wagons to transport the wounded to the hospitals. More than a hundred victims were taken to the Marine Hospital before the night was over.[32]

27. *HSCR*, 446; Chicago *Tribune*, August 8, 1866.

28. *MCR*, 262.

29. *MCR*, 262. Mayor Monroe claimed that their quick release prevented him from prosecuting those persons responsible (i.e., supporters of the convention) for the bloodshed (*GJR*, 16).

30. *HSCR*, 209; *MCR*, 263, 285. The correspondent for the *New Orleans Times* estimated that there were two hundred prisoners at the First District lockup by four o'clock that afternoon (August 1, 1866).

31. *MCR*, 285. Dr. Avery had attended to Fortune Wright at his execution.

32. *MCR*, 263, 285-86.

The Reverend Horton was one of those sent to the Marine Hospital. He had been shot in the arm at the institute and his skull had been crushed by a brick or heavy club on the way to the lockup. Horton tried to tell the doctor who admitted him about what the convention was trying to achieve. The physician, Dr. E. H. Harris, tried to stop him from talking, believing that it would hasten his death. But Horton wanted him to know what had happened, and again he tried to explain. Harris, overwhelmed by the number of serious casualties he had to attend to, paid no attention. Later, Harris could not recall any of what Horton had said.[33]

As darkness fell, some of policemen began hitting the bars, drinking hard and boasting of their kills that day. Some of them drifted down to Shinbone Alley along Victory Street (now North Peters) between Port and Lafayette (now Franklin) in the Third District, a black slum consisting of shanties along the river east of the French Quarter. About ten policemen joined by a small mob of thirty civilians and off-duty firemen knocked on doors, calling for the blacks to come out. Most of the black residents did, but Charley Johnson refused. "Are you fools?" he asked as his housemates went out. The police went in after Johnson, and people in the street heard pistol shots. The police took Johnson to the Third District lockup, where he died half an hour later.[34]

White Unionists throughout the city also had reason to be concerned. Judge Ezra Heistand had recognized this reality earlier that afternoon when he left his office to go home for dinner. Although he voiced his support for the convention during the rally Friday night, Heistand had heard enough threats to keep him away from the institute on Monday. By midafternoon he had taken a seat in the rear of a streetcar next to two acquaintances he had known for many years. The car had proceeded for several blocks and then stopped to let on a young man Heistand recognized but could not place. The man glared at him and started for a seat in the front. Suddenly, he turned. "What the hell is your hide worth today?" he demanded. "I do not know," Heistand replied, "why do you inquire?" "By God," the young man growled, "if you remain in this city until six o'clock tomorrow morning, your hide won't hold shucks."[35]

J. Randall Terry, a convention member who did not attend, sent his wife

33. *HSCR*, 37, 164, 191; Pierce, *Jotham Warren Horton*, 13.
34. *MCR*, 130, 249, 257, 278; *New Orleans Times*, August 1, 1866; *New Orleans Daily Crescent*, August 1, 1866.
35. *HSCR*, 2.

and his clerk to Colonel Lee at military headquarters to ask for protection. Colonel Lee declined, stating that the city was so dangerous that if he sent a guard, it would be attacked. But he invited Terry to the military compound for safety. Terry, his wife, and clerk set out from their store on Rampart Street about five o'clock. As they were going from Philip to Dryades through the market, they observed two policemen chasing a black man through the market. One of the officers raised his revolver and shot the man down. The second ran up to the dying man and ripped into his stomach with a long knife. Terry's party hastened on, terrified of what would happen to them should they be recognized.[36]

Thomas J. Durant had watched from his office on Carondolet between Canal and Common as the mob chased blacks down the street. He had seen Hahn escorted to the lockup, hat off and bleeding profusely, and had also watched as Fish was taken down the street in the same condition. Durant realized that his own life was at risk if he remained in the city. His fears were confirmed when a friend sent word that his life was marked.[37]

Durant sent for his carriage and had it drawn up in an alley that ran behind his office. After stopping briefly at his house, Durant drove to a plantation owned by a friend in Carrollton. Durant's friend went downtown and bought a ticket on a steamer that stopped at the plantation. Late Monday evening, Durant boarded the steamer and left. He moved his family to Washington, D.C., and sent the power of attorney to a friend, who sold his house. Durant never returned to the Crescent City.[38]

Susan Ann Crane, wife of convention member William R. Crane, was at home on the corner of Market and Annunciation when a friend of hers drove up in a carriage. Crane's friend was a Confederate sympathizer who had important information. Get your husband to leave the city, the woman told Crane, he is marked for murder. "Are you sure," Crane asked. "Yes, I am; go back and tell your husband to leave," the woman insisted. "Mr. Durant has already gone."

Crane convinced her husband to hide in the house. The time passed slowly; she was very nervous. About eleven-thirty that night she noticed five men standing on the banquette outside her front gate, one a policeman. Hoping to throw them off track, Crane went to the gate. "Gentlemen," she asked, "is there any disturbance down town?" "Yes," said a man with his hat pulled down

36. *HSCR*, 361–62.
37. *HSCR*, 8.
38. *HSCR*, 8–9; Bell, *Revolution, Romanticism, and the Afro-Creole Protest Tradition*, 262.

over his face; "they are killing niggers down in the third district." "I feel very much frightened," she replied. "My husband is out, and I feel very much frightened." "When did he go," the man with the slouched hat asked. "At dinner time," she replied. "The mayor called on all good citizens to come out and protect the city. I suppose, perhaps, he is there." "Maybe so," the man responded and moved down the street. Later, Crane saw two policemen waiting in the shadows at the corner. The moon was very bright. She waited, but all they did was watch.[39]

39. *HSCR*, 174.

13

The Rebels Have Control Here

EMMIE HORTON spent a terrible night. Monday afternoon had passed without a word from her husband, the Reverend Jotham Horton. Toward evening, a breathless messenger had arrived at their house to warn her that she would not be safe at home that night. Former rebels were searching for Unionists throughout the city, hoping to do all Yankee-lovers great harm, should they catch them, he told her. Hastily summoning her black servant, Emmie sought out a woman with whom the Hortons had boarded when they first arrived in the city. There had been a riot, a massacre, she was told when she arrived. Several young men who boarded with the woman volunteered to go out into the streets to search for Mr. Horton. They returned late that evening with news that he had been badly wounded. Emmie Horton was determined to go out and search for her husband, but darkness and the restraint of friends prevented her from going.[1]

Tuesday morning brought newspapers with the names of those arrested by the police. The Reverend Horton's name was among them with the notation that he had returned home. Emmie Horton set out for their house in Carrollton, only to return by the next streetcar. He was not there. Emmie set off im-

---

1. Pierce, *Jotham Warren Horton*, 14–20.

mediately for General Baird's headquarters. Baird recognized her and expressed surprise at her visit, telling her that he had ordered Horton's release the day before. Perhaps the reverend was still at the lockup behind City Hall, he speculated. Emmie rushed to the jail but was again disappointed. Almost in hysterics, she confronted the police clerk on duty. "Preacher Horton" had been sent to Charity Hospital, he told her. Emmie hurried off, only to be disappointed once again. The wagon carrying her husband had stopped there yesterday but had been sent on to the Marine Hospital when it appeared that black victims were also in the cart.

Emmie Horton's fears escalated. Had her husband been carried away with a load of dead bodies? Was it possible that he was still alive but soon to be buried with the other corpses? She rushed to the Marine Hospital. At the gate she was refused entrance, but catching a glimpse of Dr. E. H. Harris, the head surgeon, she called him by name and asked if her husband was there. Dr. Harris let her through the gate, and Emmie Horton rushed in among the patients and found her husband in the warden's room.

Jotham Horton was in bad shape. His eyes were swollen shut; his left arm hung useless by his side. His right arm was shattered and mangled. A wound to his chest caused by a blow from a heavy plank obstructed his breathing and made it difficult for him to speak. "Wipe my face, Emmie," he entreated. When conscious, Horton moved continually with the restless, twitching gestures of someone with neurological damage. At times, he reached out to touch his wife, whom he could not see. Most of the time, he slept a fitful sleep.

Horton lingered for six days until Sunday, August 5. That morning, the reverend remembered that he had an appointment to exchange pulpits with a black preacher in the city. "Emmie, we must send word to Bro[ther] Miles that I can't come," he told his wife. "I don't feel quite well enough to preach." Slipping into a delirium, Horton thought that he was in his own pulpit and began to pray. He announced a hymn when he finished, and Emmie joined him as he sang, her voice half choked by tears. Horton wanted to perform holy communion. Emmie tried to help as best she could. "We both drink from the same cup, Emmie," he said. He began to grow weaker. Another hymn, a benediction. "I'm going now, Emmie," he whispered. "I'm sorry you can't come with me. In the fall you'll come." That was his last connected sentence. All he could utter now were incoherent syllables of a prayer. "In the vale—the vale—home yonder—good by." At six o'clock that evening, the Reverend Jotham Warren Horton died.

Chief Adams reported to Dr. Albert Hartsuff, surgeon at Sedwick Military Hospital, that twenty-two policemen had been wounded during the riot. Most of the wounded had been treated at Dr. W. H. Berthelot's office on Canal Street before returning home. Wanting to see for himself, Dr. Hartsuff visited the homes of the wounded policemen but found that only a few had been injured and that most of them had already returned to duty. Dr. Hartsuff concluded that instead of twenty-two, only ten officers had been wounded during the fracas, two seriously. Policeman Mark Sokolowsky had a pistol ball in the side; Policeman J. W. Hennessy suffered from a severe blow to the head. There had been one fatality. Corporal Walgamoth from the First District had died of sunstroke brought on by excitement and the heat. Also, a white civilian had been killed. Edgar Henry Cenas, a student at the Medical College next to the institute, had been struck in the neck by a stray shot when he ventured outside to see what the commotion was all about.[2]

It was the duty of the parish coroner to determine how many blacks had been killed or wounded, but he found that doing so was next to impossible. At the workhouse he discovered 22 bodies of black men stretched out on the ground. He conducted autopsies on 5 additional victims (3 black and 2 white), among them Constance Loup. His final report included a list of 155 known casualties, most of whom had been admitted to the Marine Hospital.[3]

Dr. Harris, head surgeon for the Freedmen's Bureau at the Marine Hospital, admitted 102 black patients on Monday and 6 more on Tuesday, mostly young men in their late teens or early twenties, with contusions, fractures, and pistol wounds. This number did not include either Horton or John Henderson, the only two white patients taken there. Over the next three days, 14 of the 108 died, and many others were discharged to the care of friends or family. The estimate of casualties based on the records at the Marine Hospital is probably low because it does not account for many blacks wounded during the riot who were taken home and cared for until they healed or died.[4]

The number of dead and wounded will never be known with certainty.

2. *HSCR*, 81, 181; *MCR*, 171, 267; *New Orleans Daily Crescent*, August 1, 1866; *New Orleans Times*, July 31, August 1, 1866.

3. *HSCR*, 182–86. The workhouse was a minimum security prison where unemployed blacks were sent to serve time for vagrancy (see, e.g., "Grand Jury," *New Orleans Daily Crescent*, January 10, 1866).

4. Morning Report of Sick and Wounded for July 31, 1866; Report by the Officer of the Day on the Condition of the Hospital, December 1865–August 1868, for July 31 and August 1, 1866, Records of the Freedmen's Hospital and New Orleans Area Field Offices of the Bureau of Refugees, Freedmen, and Abandoned Lands, 1865–1869, M-1483, rolls 3 and 1, respectively, NA; *HSCR*, 81, 190. The Morning Report lists 104 names admitted as a result of the riot. Of these, 27 (26 percent) were in their teens, 46 (44 percent) in their twenties, 18 (17 percent) in their thirties, 11 (10 percent) in their forties, one age fifty-seven, and one age sixty.

Surgeon Hartsuff's official tally, which was appended to Baird's report to the military commission, counted "thirty-seven certainly, and ten more probably, killed on the side of the convention, against a single citizen [Cenas] on the side of the city authorities." Hartsuff also noted that although forty-eight men siding with the convention had been severely wounded, there was "not a single man in that category upon the other side." In addition, the surgeon was able to document "eighty-eight certain, and twenty more probably, cases of slight wounds among friends of the convention, and but ten such cases among the police and its friends." Hartsuff concluded that this disparity in the number of killed and wounded was "highly significant."[5]

Jean-Charles Houzeau went to the offices of the *New Orleans Tribune* at No. 21 Conti on Tuesday, expecting to find the presses destroyed but instead found a company of black soldiers from the 81st Infantry, United States Colored Troops, standing on guard. The staff had fled, save one, and the typesetters were gone as well. There would not be an edition of the *Tribune* in the foreseeable future.[6]

The *Tribune* had been an outspoken advocate for universal male suffrage for the past two years. The paper had also called for the right of blacks to serve on juries, to ride on nonsegregated streetcars, to attend integrated schools, and to eat in restaurants and attend the theater without discrimination. Houzeau had joined the *Tribune* as its new editor in November 1864. A Belgian-born journalist, naturalist, and astronomer, Houzeau had questioned whether reconvening the convention was legal, but he was interested in the larger question: who determines who can vote? Houzeau, in fact, had an answer: the convention should be allowed to reconvene, endorse universal male suffrage, and then let the matter be decided in the United States Congress. According to this scenario, reconvening the convention would force Congress to determine suffrage on a national scale and thus avoid the problems resulting from the granting of suffrage on a piecemeal basis from state to state.[7] With the convention smashed and the supporters of universal male suffrage in disarray, Houzeau's solution was a moot point.

5. Baird, Appendix O to the Board of Investigation report *MCR*, 93.
6. Houzeau to Auguste Houzeau, August 5, 1866, in Houzeau, *My Passage*, 159.
7. Rankin, "Introduction" to Houzeau, *My Passage*, 23–29; Houzeau, *My Passage*, 124; also Bell, *Revolution, Romanticism, and the Afro-Creole Protest Tradition*, 252, and Connor, "Reconstruction Rebels," 159–81. Although Houzeau and nearly a quarter of the *Tribune*'s employees were white, the leadership and the money men behind the paper were free blacks (see Rankin's footnote in Houzeau, *My Passage*, 25). Paul Trévigne, editor of *L'Union* and the *Tribune*'s first editor, continued under Houzeau as associate editor (Connor, "Reconstruction Rebels," 164–65).

Houzeau sat at his desk, writing down what had happened as best he could remember, first in English and then in French. Next he drafted a succession of telegrams and letters, informing friends in the North of the events of the previous day. "Ces esclavagistes sont des démons," he wrote an acquaintance. What was needed now, Houzeau asserted, was an "iron hand" to eradicate racial prejudice. Houzeau did not forget the Radicals in Congress to whom he had faithfully sent every issue of the *Tribune* and drafted a report for them too.[8]

The *Tribune* was the only local outlet for disseminating the convention's side of the story, and as the day drew on, supporters of the convention came to the *Tribune* office to confer with Houzeau. Patiently, Houzeau drew up a list of witnesses to send to Washington. He also sent the names to Baird. Houzeau was certain that the army would make an investigation.[9]

Dr. Dostie was at the Hotel Dieu, an infirmary run by the Sisters of Charity on the corner of Common and Johnson Streets. Private rooms cost between $4 and $7 per day.[10] Dostie did not concern himself with the expense, for he did not have long to live.

Dostie lay on a hospital bed. Both eyes were black; his face was cut and swollen. He could not move in any direction. On Tuesday, Colonel DeWitt Clinton of Baird's staff visited Dostie in his room. How is John Henderson, Dostie asked the colonel? He is dead, Clinton told him. Dostie paused for a moment before remarking, "Well, it is a strange coincidence. We were born upon the same day, and embarked in the same glorious cause. I had reason to be apprehensive—to fear a bloody attack—but not he. Strange."[11]

Four officers appointed by Baird to investigate the riot went to the Hotel Dieu two days later to obtain Dostie's statement. He gave it in a detailed, matter-of-fact manner. Supporters of the convention had not expected violence. "One fool of a negro" had fired once, he said, but the police had initiated the

8. Houzeau to N. C. Schmit, July 31, 1866, quoted by Rankin in "Introduction" to Houzeau, *My Passage*, 63; Houzeau to Auguste Houzeau, August 5, 1866, ibid., 159.

9. Houzeau to Auguste Houzeau, August 5, 1866, ibid., 159. The *Tribune* resumed printing within the month with the following motto displayed prominently on the front page: "To Every Citizen His Rights: Universal Suffrage. Equality Before the Law. To Every Laborer His Due: An Equitable Salary. Eight Hours a Legal Day's Work" (*New Orleans Tribune*, August 31, 1866).

10. Advertisement for the Hotel Dieu in *Gardner's New Orleans Directory for 1867*, xxiv.

11. *New Orleans Times*, August 2, 1866. Clinton was in error. John Henderson lingered for six weeks before dying on September 13, 1866 (*HSCR*, 192, and *New Orleans Times*, September 14, 1866).

attack. They had barricaded the door to buy time until the army arrived. Dostie described the man who had shot him in the back. "He had dark eyes, black eyebrows, black side whiskers, a mustache—not large, and black hair. His teeth were broken." That was the extent of what Dostie had to say.[12]

Dostie lingered for another two days. Friends who called on him found a smile on his lips. "I think I shall outlive this," he told one visitor, "but if I don't, I think justice will be rendered hereafter." Dostie died on August 5.[13]

Andrew S. Herron, the attorney general for the state of Louisiana and formerly a Confederate officer during the Civil War, approached Baird on Tuesday to gain the cooperation of the army in arresting members of the convention who had assembled at the Mechanics' Institute. Baird was not interested. Herron showed the general a telegram he had received from President Johnson the day before. "You will call on General Sheridan, or whoever may be in command," Johnson wrote, "for sufficient force to sustain the civil authority in suppressing all illegal or unlawful assemblies which usurp or assume to exercise any power or authority without first having obtained the consent of the people of the State." Johnson's position was clear. "If there is to be a convention, let it be composed of delegates chosen fresh from the people of the whole state. Usurpation will not be tolerated."[14]

Herron assumed that Baird would cooperate on the strength of Johnson's telegram alone, but Baird demurred. Sheridan was still out of town, but he expected his commanding officer any minute. Furthermore, neither Johnson nor Stanton had seen fit to send Baird instructions directly. Baird decided that it would be better to wait and let Sheridan, the commander of the department, decide to what degree the army would cooperate with the grand jury.[15]

Sheridan returned from Texas just before midnight on Tuesday and found the city in a state of great excitement. Rumors of a black insurrection were rampant. Whites were in the streets; many were armed. Blacks stayed in their houses, fearing further attacks by the police or civilians. Some whites, exhila-

---

12. *MCR*, 108–9.

13. *HSCR*, 160; Reed, *Life of A. P. Dostie*, 318; New Orleans Health Department, "Death Certificates, as kept by the Recorder of Births, Marriages, and Deaths," vol. 34 (1866), New Orleans City Hall.

14. *HSCR*, 244–45; Johnson to Herron, July 30, 1866, in *MCR*, 5. Herron served as a captain in the 7th Louisiana Infantry under Colonel Harry T. Hays, the sheriff of Orleans Parish who hoped to arrest the conventioneers (Arthur W. Bergeron, *Guide to Louisiana Confederate Military Units, 1861–1865* [Baton Rouge: Louisiana State University Press, 1989], 87).

15. *HSCR*, 244.

rated by their participation in the carnage on the day before, vowed to drive the Union army, particularly the hated black soldiers of the 81st Infantry, out of the city. Sheridan learned of the threats as soon as he arrived and reacted swiftly. Keeping the 1st Infantry and the battery of artillery on alert in Lafayette Square, he ordered the 81st Infantry to leave its barracks and occupy the Custom House. With its massive granite walls, the Custom House was a natural fortification. The 81st Infantry would not be intimidated there.[16]

Although he was fatigued by his journey, Sheridan sat down and composed a telegram to his commander, Ulysses S. Grant, which he sent the next day.

GENERAL:

You are doubtless aware of the serious riot which occurred in this city on the 30th. A political body styling itself the convention of 1864, met on the 30th, for as it is alleged, the purpose of remodeling the present constitution of the State. The leaders were political agitators and revolutionary men, and the action of the convention was liable to induce breaches of the public peace.

I had made up my mind to arrest the head men, if the proceedings of the convention were calculated to disturb the tranquillity of the department; but I had no case for action until they committed the overt act. In the meantime, official duty called me to Texas, and the Mayor of the City, during my absence, suppressed the convention by the use of their police force, and in so doing, attacked members of the convention and a party of 200 negroes, with fire-arms, clubs, and knives in a manner so unnecessary and atrocious as to compel me to say that it was murder.[17]

Sheridan had a preliminary report ready for President Johnson a week later. Starting with a review of the speeches and language at the rally on the Friday night before the convention, Sheridan gave an evenhanded account of the events transpiring on Monday, July 30, 1866. "The immediate cause of this terrible affair was the assemblage of this Convention," he reported. "The remote cause," he continued, "was the bitter and antagonistic feeling which has been growing in this community since the advent of the present mayor, who in the organization of the police force selected many desperate men, and some of them known murderers." Noting that although "no steps have as yet been

16. *HSCR*, 347–49; *MCR*, 183–84; *New Orleans Daily Crescent*, August 1, 1866.
17. *MCR*, 9.

taken by the civil authorities to arrest citizens who were engaged in this massacre, or policemen who perpetuated such cruelties," Sheridan reported that members of the convention had been arrested and freed on bail. Abell was to blame for this state of affairs, Sheridan believed. "Judge Abell whose course I have closely watched for nearly a year, I now consider one of the most dangerous men we have here to the peace and quiet of the city." But with his usual disdain for both sides, Sheridan also had harsh words for members of the convention. "The leading men of the Convention, King Cutler, Hahn, and others, have been political agitators and are bad men." He did not stop there. "I regret to say that the course of Governor Wells has been vacillating," Sheridan added, "and that during the late troubles, he has shown very little of the man."

Sheridan continued, "It is useless to attempt to disguise the hostility that exists on the part of a great many here towards northern men, and this unfortunate affair has so precipitated matters that there is now a test of what shall be the status of northern men." He knew what was in store. "If this matter is permitted to pass over without a thorough and determined prosecution of those engaged in it, we may look out for frequent scenes of the same kind, not only here but in other places."[18] Sheridan was more right than he could possibly know.

Judge Edmund Abell assembled the sixteen members of the grand jury on Thursday, August 2, to investigate the nature and cause of the riot. Baird had blocked Abell's attempt to have Sheriff Hays arrest the members of the convention on Monday afternoon, but the charge in those indictments was unlawful assembly, "dangerous to the peace and good order of the State." Because there had actually been a riot, the charge would now be more serious. "Whoever shall make or assist at any riot, rout, or unlawful assembly," Abell told the members of the jury, "shall suffer fine or imprisonment, or both, at the discretion of the court. I charge you, gentlemen," he stated, "if any one of these offenses has been committed, all who shall have made or knowingly assisted are guilty as principals, and, as such, are liable for all the criminal consequences that follow."[19]

Dutifully, the grand jury began calling witnesses. By the end of the next week, they were finished. Twenty-nine witnesses testified—Mayor Monroe, Lieutenant Governor Voorhies, Chief Adams, several policemen, and several

18. Sheridan to Andrew Johnson, August 6, 1866, in Philip Sheridan Papers, container 52, reel 47, pp. 415–20; also in MCR, 13–14.
19. HSCR, 275, 279.

white citizens. Their stories were remarkably consistent, even down to the smallest details. The blacks had started it. Their behavior had been belligerent, and they had fired the first shots. The police had done their best to maintain order and had tried to protect their prisoners after arresting them. A few white men in the crowd had gotten out of hand, but their behavior was no worse than that of blacks in the procession or the crowd in front of the institute. The grand jury did not call any blacks to testify, or any members of the convention, or anyone who was present in the hall.[20]

The grand jury's report placed blame for the riot squarely at the feet of the convention delegates, "political tricksters," as it called them, who had attempted "to deprive us of our proper participation in our own government." The grand jury also found fault with Governor Wells. "We find him co-operating with the usurping convention," read the report, "for the purpose of destroying the government under which he holds his power and position." As far as blacks were concerned, the members of the jury concluded that they had fallen victim "to the lawless ambition for place and power of bad and unscrupulous white men." Not surprisingly, the grand jury voted to indict all those who had been present at the roll call. None of the police, not one white citizen, was charged.[21]

Unionists throughout the city were completely demoralized by the riot. "The rebels have control here and are determined to maintain it," Judge Howell wrote Nathaniel P. Banks in Washington on August 2. "The members of the convention who were present on Monday are indicted by a packed rebel grand jury at the charge of a rebel Judge [Abell] and under the direction of a rebel Attorney General [Herron] on the charge of making and knowingly assisting at an unlawful assembly. We will be tried by a rebel jury," Howell continued, "& of course found guilty & handed over to a rebel Sheriff [Hays]." Howell had reason to be alarmed. Lucien Adams was hanging around his house, keeping watch.[22]

There were other blows to Unionist hopes for the Free State of Louisiana in the days that followed. Rufus K. Howell had traveled to Washington in early July to seek support for the reconvening of the convention. In private, many of the Republican congressmen had encouraged Judge Howell, and eventually, a caucus of congressional Republicans had met to discuss the situa-

20. *GJR*, 3–17.
21. *GJR*, 2–3; *HSCR*, 246.
22. *HSCR*, 48; *MCR*, 14; Howell to Banks, August 2, 1866, Banks Collection.

tion. George S. Boutwell, a Radical member of Congress from Massachusetts, had addressed the group, telling them of a meeting scheduled for July 30 and urging them to consider throwing their support behind the move to amend the Louisiana constitution to allow black males to vote. It was even rumored that several influential leaders in Congress had written a letter to Howell indicating their support.[23]

Now that the riot had occurred, these same congressmen rushed to distance themselves from the convention. The following question was put to Henry T. Blow, congressman from Missouri and member of the House Select Committee on Reconstruction:

> It has been put in evidence that a letter was written before the assembling of the convention in New Orleans in July last, by one or more members of the Reconstruction Committee, to Mr. Flanders in New Orleans, or some other person, expressing some opinion in regard to the action of Congress, or giving some advice, or making some suggestions, concerning the proposed convention, and saying what Congress might or might not do in a certain case; please state if you wrote such a letter, or any letter, or know of any such letter being written by your committee, or any member of it?

Representative Blow was quick to answer: "I wrote no such letter; have no knowledge of such a letter being written, and, in fact, know nothing in connection with the subject at all."[24]

And so it went. Six senators and thirteen representatives from the Thirty-ninth Congress were called, and each denied that he had encouraged the delegates' plans to reconvene. Of the nineteen, less than half admitted to having met with Howell during his visit to Washington. Collectively, they had a terrible memory. In response to questions concerning his possible role in giving Howell hope that Congress might intervene by recognizing the work of the convention, Boutwell answered, "I do not recollect," fourteen times. He was confident in answering only one question: "Are you a member of the Joint Committee on Reconstruction?" "Yes," Boutwell replied. None of the other members were any more helpful.[25]

23. *HSCR*, 540–41; *New York Times*, July 12, 15, 1866.

24. *HSCR*, 545–46.

25. Testimony of Senators Jacob M. Howard, W. P. Fessenden, George H. Williams, Reverdy Johnson, J. W. Grimes, and Ira Harris; Representatives George S. Boutwell, Thaddeus Stevens, Elihu B. Washburne, Elijah Hise, Justin S. Morrill, Andrew J. Rogers, Josiah B. Grinnell,

This was not as Judge Howell had remembered it. He recalled encouragement, although the members of Congress whom he approached were careful to emphasize that as individuals they could not speak for Congress as a whole. "We cannot promise you anything," he recalled their saying, "but if your people adopt a constitution with the principles you mention embodied in it, we will entertain it as favorably as we can as individual members of Congress." Howell had left Washington convinced that there were no legal barriers to what he proposed. Now, in his greatest hour of need, none of those Howell had counted on came forward.[26]

Coming as it did on the heels of similar eruptions in Memphis and Charleston, the New Orleans riot increased the perception in the North that white southerners were determined to unleash a reign of terror on the recently emancipated slaves. The barrage of self-congratulatory editorials in southern newspapers, which praised whites in New Orleans for giving a "salutary warning" that the South would never submit to Yankee rule, strengthened this conviction and persuaded northern voters that the South had refused to accept the verdict arrived at by four years of a bloody war.[27]

The riot in New Orleans also discredited Andrew Johnson's policy regarding Reconstruction. Hoping to diminish his presidential powers further, Congress passed the Tenure of Office Act in March 1867. The act required the president to obtain the Senate's consent for removals or appointments to any federal office, including his cabinet. This restriction presented a particular problem for Johnson in regard to Edwin Stanton, the secretary of war. Johnson had never forgiven Stanton for withholding Baird's telegram. In addition, Johnson was aware of other things the secretary of war had done to undermine his office, such as leaking confidential information from cabinet meetings.[28]

Some of Johnson's supporters urged the president to remove Stanton and declare the Tenure of Office Act null and void. But Johnson wanted to avoid a showdown and decided to take advantage of a provision in the act that would allow him to suspend Stanton while Congress was out of session. Therefore, Johnson waited until the summer recess in 1867 and then dismissed Stanton,

---

William D. Kelley, Daniel Morris, Roscoe Conkling, John A. Bingham, Nathaniel P. Banks, Henry J. Raymond, and Henry J. Blow, all in *HSCR*, 486–91, 500–504, 540–46.

26. *HSCR*, 56–57.

27. W. R. Brock, *An American Crisis: Congress and Reconstruction, 1865–1867* (New York: Harper Torchbooks, 1963), 158–59; Carter, *When the War Was Over*, 249–53; see also Tunnell, *Crucible of Reconstruction*, 106–7.

28. Foner, *Reconstruction*, 333–34; Sefton, *Andrew Johnson*, 159.

replacing him with Ulysses S. Grant. When the House reconvened in November, the Judiciary Committee voted to impeach the president, but the motion failed on the floor. Vindicated, or so he thought, Johnson delivered a message on Stanton's suspension five days later. Of the many complaints Johnson could have voiced to justify Stanton's removal, the president chose to emphasize the tardy telegram. Johnson felt that he had been blamed, unfairly, for the violence in New Orleans and wanted to use this opportunity to set the record straight.[29]

Then the unexpected happened. Grant resigned his appointment as secretary of war and returned to his duties as commanding general of the army, which put Stanton back at work in his old office. After considering his options for several weeks, Johnson decided on February 21, 1868, to remove Stanton once again. The Senate quickly passed a resolution stating that Johnson did not have the authority to dismiss Stanton, and the House voted three days later to impeach the president.[30]

The trial began in the Senate on March 23 and lasted more than seven weeks. Finally, on May 16, the chief justice called for a vote on the strongest of the charges in the bills of indictment. Needing a two-thirds majority, the Senate failed to convict by one vote, thirty-five to nineteen. Seven Republican senators sacrificed their political careers by voting not guilty.[31] Although Johnson survived impeachment, his political future had been ruined. Six months later Ulysses S. Grant was elected president of the United States.

With the president's plan for Reconstruction in disarray, the Radicals passed a series of bills that gave Congress control of the process. Among other things, these laws mandated that every southern state had to accept universal male suffrage as a condition for readmission to the Union. Louisiana dutifully convened another constitutional convention and adopted a new constitution giving blacks the right to vote and hold office. The document was ratified in April 1868, and Louisiana rejoined her sister states in the Union shortly thereafter.[32]

Ironically, the violent reaction of whites in New Orleans had accomplished precisely what the advocates of black suffrage wanted all along. But their victory was short-lived. By 1877, former Confederates had reestablished them-

29. Sefton, *Andrew Johnson*, 160–61, 167–68; Secretary of War, *Suspension of Stanton*, passim. The Supreme Court eventually ruled that the Tenure of Office Act was unconstitutional in the case of *Myers v. United States*.
30. Sefton, *Andrew Johnson*, 172–73.
31. Ibid., 179–80.
32. Tunnell, *Crucible of Reconstruction*, 5; Uzee, "Beginnings of the Louisiana Republican Party," 209–11; Vandal, "Origins of the New Orleans Riot," 135.

selves as a political force in Louisiana. In the decade that followed, white Lou-isianians tightened their control over the state's black citizens. "For the first time since the war," a white New Orleanian boasted in 1888, "we've got the nigger where we want him." By 1898, when the state adopted another consti-tution, blacks in Louisiana lost all the political privileges they had achieved, including the right to vote. This time, however, the North turned its back. Administrative inefficiency on the part of the federal government, the consti-tutional conservatism of Americans in general, and racism in the North and South doomed the attempt to establish a new social order based on the prin-ciple that all men are equal before the law.[33]

It has been said that the South lost the war but won the peace.[34] That state-ment applied only to white southerners, however, for blacks in the South were the real losers. Disfranchised, terrorized, and marginalized, black southerners had to wait for more than a century before the events set in motion by the riot in New Orleans on July 30, 1866, were put to rest.[35]

33. R. C. Hitchcock to George Washington Cable, September 1, 1888, quoted in Dale A. Somers, "Black and White in New Orleans: A Study in Urban Race Relations, 1865–1900," *Journal of Southern History* 40 (February 1974): 42; Anthony, "Negro Creole Community ," 44; Foner, *Reconstruction*, 590–96; Gillette, *Retreat from Reconstruction*, 363–67; Ripley, *Slaves and Freed-men*, 199; Taylor, *Louisiana Reconstructed*, 507–8.

34. Gillette, *Retreat from Reconstruction*, 378–80; Grantham, *Life and Death of the Solid South*, 33. Gillette noted: "The irony was not merely that the South had lost the war and won the peace by nullifying Reconstruction, but that it was actually rewarded through congressional apportionment, when the southern states gained more congressional seats and more electoral votes, by having counted the entire free black population, yet prevented the blacks from voting" (p. 378). Before emancipation, one slave was tabulated in the census as equal to three-fifths of a white person for the purpose of determining the apportionment of seats in the United States Congress.

35. Rable, *But There Was No Peace*, 43, 58. For an exhaustive account of white-on-black vio-lence following the Civil War, see Allen W. Trelease, *White Terror: The Ku Klux Klan Conspiracy and Southern Reconstruction* (Baton Rouge: Louisiana State University Press, 1971).

Postscript

EW OF THE PEOPLE who played a major role in the New Orleans riot survived in office for very long after the dust settled. General Absalom Baird was the first to go. Although Sheridan believed that Baird's indecision had contributed to the outburst, the commanding general remained silent as criticism mounted. Nevertheless, Baird saw the handwriting on the wall and resigned his post as director the Freedmen's Bureau in Louisiana on September 8, 1866. Nine days later he asked for and was granted an extended leave from the army and left the state. But Baird was too good an officer to be shunted aside entirely, and he went on to complete a successful military career as a staff officer in the inspector general's office. The highlight of that career came in 1885 when he was named inspector general of the United States Army. Absalom Baird died in 1905.[1]

The Reconstruction Acts in 1867 gave Sheridan the authority to replace local officials, which he used on March 27 to remove Mayor John T. Monroe and Judge Edmund Abell from their respective offices. Monroe left the city and moved to Savannah, Georgia, where he lived in obscurity until his death

---

1. *New Orleans Republican*, September 6, 1867; Dawson, *Army Generals and Reconstruction*, 42; Warner, *Generals in Blue*, 16.

in 1874. Judge Abell had better luck. Running for and winning reelection to his old seat on the bench, Abell continued to preside over the First District court until a change in the state constitution made judgeships subject to appointment by the governor. Abell practiced law in the Crescent City until his death from cancer in 1884.[2]

J. Madison Wells continued to serve as governor despite Sheridan's contempt for the indecisive politician. Uncooperative and contentious, Wells finally irritated Sheridan to the point that he decided on June 3, 1867, to boot him out of office. White Louisianians generally applauded Sheridan's action, for the wily governor had alienated almost everyone. "All's well that ends Wells," a headline in the *New Orleans Times* quipped in reporting his removal.[3]

Sheridan had the authority to appoint Wells's successor because the state was still under military control. Initially, Sheridan offered the posts to Thomas J. Durant, who refused, preferring to remain in Washington. In his stead, Sheridan appointed Benjamin F. Flanders, who moved into the governor's office on June 8, much to Wells's chagrin.[4]

Out of office and impoverished by the destruction of his property by Union troops during their two forays up the Red River, Wells played only a minor role in the waning days of Reconstruction, first as a member of the electoral returning board and later as surveyor of customs. He spent the latter part of his life trying, unsuccessfully, to get the federal government to reimburse him for his wartime losses. Wells died in February 1899 at the age of ninety-nine.[5]

The next to go was Chief of Police Thomas Adams, ostensibly because of his pro-Confederate convictions. Neither the new mayor, who initiated the dismissal, nor Sheridan, who issued the order, gave a reason for Adams's termination. Although Chief Adams soon faded from public view, his namesake, Lucien Adams, did not. Active in seeking to prevent carpetbaggers and scalawags from holding positions of influence in the Crescent City, Adams was involved in several racial disturbances during Reconstruction. Turning his attention to the practice of law once the conservatives had regained control of

2. Joseph G. Dawson, "General Phil Sheridan and Military Reconstruction in Louisiana," *Civil War History* 24 (June 1978): 134–35; Dawson, *Army Generals and Reconstruction*, 47; Taylor, *Louisiana Reconstructed*, 153; *New York Times*, August 10, 1884. Sheridan also removed Attorney General Andrew Herron.

3. *New Orleans Times*, June 4, 1867; Dawson, "General Phil Sheridan," 141; Dawson, *Army Generals and Reconstruction*, 53.

4. Dawson, "General Phil Sheridan," 142; Dawson, *Army Generals and Reconstruction*, 54.

5. Lowrey, "Political Career of James Madison Wells," 1108–15.

the state government, Adams was appointed to fill the unexpired term as chief of police in 1885. He died in 1900, "active and vigorous" to the end.[6]

Ironically, General Philip Sheridan did not last much longer than the men he replaced. Andrew Johnson disliked Sheridan's close ties to the Radicals and his aggressive interference in local affairs. Johnson removed Sheridan from office in August 1867 and replaced him with Joseph A. Mower.[7]

Once in command, Mower decided to finish the work that Sheridan had started by ousting Sheriff Harry Hays, Lieutenant Governor Albert Voorhies, and most of the remaining pro-Confederate officials. They were an "impediment to Reconstruction," Mower explained in justifying the removals. Hays continued to resist Reconstruction generally and black civil rights in particular for the next ten years until he died of Bright's disease in 1876. Voorhies remained active in state politics, serving as district attorney of St. Martin Parish and gaining election to the state senate in 1872. He later prepared a revision of the Louisiana Civil Code and continued to work in criminal jurisprudence until his death in 1913 at the age of eighty-four.[8]

Most of the members of the convention who survived the riot never captured the attention or enthusiasm they had generated while making plans to enfranchise black men in their bid to remain in power. Finding himself "scoffed & scorned" and his "business lost," R. King Cutler left New Orleans and returned to the North, where he died in obscurity. Rufus K. Howell retained his seat on the Louisiana Supreme Court until conservatives recaptured the reins of state government and ousted him in 1877.[9]

Of all of the convention supporters, the agile Michael Hahn survived with the greatest success. After editing the *New Orleans Republican* for several years, Hahn moved to St. Charles Parish and founded the town of Hahnville. The new streets bore names with personal connections. Hahn named one after himself and three others after his friends: Dostie, Shaw, and Lincoln. During the 1870s, Hahn served as a district judge in the federal courts, state registrar of voters, and speaker of the Louisiana House of Representatives. In 1884, he was elected to the United States Congress and moved to Washington, where he spent the last two years of his life. "In his death," the *New York Times* noted in 1886, "the last white republican Congressman is eliminated from the late

6. Rousey, *Policing a Southern City*, 123; *New Orleans Daily Picayune*, August 10, 1867, March 2, 1900.

7. Dawson, *Army Generals and Reconstruction*, 57–63.

8. Ibid., 47; Conrad, ed., *Dictionary of Louisiana Biography*, 1:386, 2:815–16; "Judge Voorhies Sinks to Sleep," *New Orleans Daily Picayune*, January 21, 1913.

9. Conrad, ed., *Dictionary of Louisiana Biography*, 1:206, 412.

Confederate States south of Virginia." The article in the *Times* was more than a notice of Michael Hahn's death; it was the obituary for an era.[10]

The Mechanics' Institute continued to serve as the state's temporary capital until the state government was moved back to Baton Rouge in 1879. Three years later, a wealthy businessman, Paul Tulane, made a large donation to the University of Louisiana, which was located next to the institute on the corner of Common and Dryades. Needing a building for its new academic programs, trustees of the university purchased the institute and named it Tulane Hall. They also changed the name of the university to honor its generous benefactor.[11]

In 1893, Tulane University relocated uptown to the present campus on St. Charles near Carrollton and moved the law department into the recently vacated Tulane Hall. The law school operated in the building until 1903, when it was also moved to the new campus. Wishing to dispose of its property at the downtown location, Tulane sold the Mechanics' Institute to the Grunewald Hotel, which had been built in 1893 on Baronne Street directly behind the old building. In 1908, the new owners demolished the institute and erected a fourteen-story annex facing Dryades (now called University Place). Fifteen years later, the Grunewald Hotel was sold, and its name was changed to the Roosevelt Hotel in honor of President Theodore Roosevelt.[12]

The general manager of the Roosevelt Hotel was Seymour Weiss, a friend and confidant of Huey P. Long. After he became governor in 1928, Long rented a suite of rooms in the Roosevelt and stayed there whenever he came to New Orleans. Oral tradition has it that one of the nightspots Long liked best was the Blue Room in the Roosevelt Hotel.[13]

The Blue Room was a famous supper club. Over the years, it hosted per-

10. Michael Hahn obituary, *New York Times*, March 16, 1886. Today, only Hahn and Lincoln remain. Dostie and Shaw Streets have been renamed Pine and Elm (Simpson and Baker, "Michael Hahn," 230).

11. Joe Gray Taylor, *Louisiana: A Bicentennial History* (New York: Norton in association with the American Association for State and Local History, 1976), 119, 135; Taylor, *Louisiana Reconstructed*, 216, 226, 245–46, 248–49, 253; John P. Dyer, *Tulane: The Biography of a University, 1834–1965* (New York: Harper & Row, 1966), 11–15, 38, 52, 150; Beatrice M. Field, "Potpourri: An Assortment of Tulane's People and Places" (New Orleans: Tulane Library Special Collections typescript, August 1983), 82.

12. Dyer, *Tulane*, 68, 117; "Location Sites." *Savor the Regions*. 1998. http://www.lpb.org/programs/savor/ locations_300.html (December 5, 1998). The Grunewald Hotel was built in 1893.

13. T. Harry Williams, *Huey Long* (New York: Knopf, 1969), 318, 374–75, 429, 435.

formances by some of the finest musical artists of the era, such as Tony Bennett, Marlene Dietrich, and Mel Torme. In the 1950s, radio station WWL began a series of nationwide broadcasts from the Blue Room, increasing its reputation as one of the finest entertainment venues in the country.[14] It is doubtful, however, that the men and women who resonated to the sounds of Dixeland, jazz, and big band music in the Blue Room during its heyday realized that they were dancing where the Mechanics' Institute once stood.

In 1965, the Roosevelt Hotel was purchased and renamed once again, this time as the Fairmont-Roosevelt and later the Fairmont Hotel, under which name it operates today. Each year thousands of tourists step out of buses, cabs, and cars at the front entrance of the Fairmont.[15] But there is no plaque to commemorate the New Orleans riot or to honor the dead. There is no indication that the worst act of violence in the city's history occurred at that place many, many years ago.

14. "The History of the Fairmont." *Fairmont Hotel.* http://www.neworleansonline.com/fairmont.htm (December 5, 1998).

15. John Churchill Chase, *Frenchmen, Desire, Good Children, and Other Streets of New Orleans,* 3d ed. (New York: Simon & Schuster, 1997), 62.

Bibliography

MANUSCRIPTS

Library of Congress, Washington, D.C.
    Banks, Nathaniel P. Collection.
    Butler, Benjamin F. Papers.
    Chase, Salmon P. Papers.
    Johnson, Andrew. Presidential Collection
    Lincoln, Abraham. Papers.
    Quincy, Wendell, Holmes and Upham Family Papers.
    Schurz, Carl. Papers.
    Sheridan, Philip H. Papers.
    Trumbull, Lyman. Papers.
New Orleans Public Library, New Orleans, La. City Archives.
New York Historical Society, New York, N.Y.
    Durant, Thomas J. Papers.
    "Minutes of General Committee of Union Associations, May 19, 1863."
Southern Historical Society Papers, University of North Carolina, Chapel Hill, N.C.
    Warmoth, Henry Clay. Papers.

GOVERNMENT DOCUMENTS

Acts Passed by the General Assembly of the State of Louisiana, Extra Session, 1865. New Orleans: J. O. Nixon, 1866.
Debates in the Convention for the Revision and Amendment of the Constitution of the State of Louisiana, 1864. New Orleans: W. R. Fish, 1864.
Grand Jury Report, and the Evidence Taken by Them in Reference to the Great Riot in

New Orleans, Louisiana, July 30, 1866. New Orleans: Daily Crescent Office, [1866?].

House Executive Documents No. 68: New Orleans Riots, 39th Cong., 2d sess. Washington, D.C.: U.S.Government Printing Office, 1866.

House Report No. 16: Report of the Select Committee on New Orleans Riots. 39th Cong., 2d sess. Washington, D.C.: U.S. Government Printing Office, 1867; reprint, Freeport, N.Y.: Books for Libraries Press, 1971.

Journal of the House of Representatives of the State of Louisiana, Extra Session, November 23, 1865. New Orleans: J. O. Nixon, 1865.

Secretary of War. *Message of the President of the United States and the Report of the Committee on Military Affairs, Etc., in Regard to the Suspension of Hon. E. M. Stanton*. Washington, D.C.: U.S. Government Printing Office, 1868.

THESES AND DISSERTATIONS

Anthony, Arthé Agnes. "The Negro Creole Community in New Orleans, 1880–1920: An Oral History." Ph.D. dissertation, University of California, Irvine, 1978.

Herbert, Mary Jacqueline. "John T. Monroe: Race, Politics, and the Police in New Orleans, 1858–1866." M.A. thesis, University of New Orleans, 1991.

Leavens, Finian P. "*L'Union* and the New Orleans *Tribune* and Louisiana Reconstruction." M.A. thesis, Louisiana State University, 1966.

Messner, William F. "The Federal Army and Blacks in the Department of the Gulf, 1862–1865." Ph.D. dissertation, University of Wisconsin, 1972.

Vandal, Gilles. "The New Orleans Riot of 1866: The Anatomy of a Tragedy." Ph.D. dissertation, College of William and Mary, 1978.

NEWSPAPERS

Boston Daily Journal, 1864

Chicago Tribune, 1866

New Orleans Bee, 1866

New Orleans Daily Crescent, 1860, 1865–66

New Orleans Daily Delta, 1861–62

New Orleans Daily Picayune, 1860, 1862–66, 1900, 1913

New Orleans Daily Southern Star, 1865–66

New Orleans Daily True Delta, 1860, 1862, 1864–66

New Orleans Deutsche Zeitung, 1866

New Orleans Era, 1863–64

New Orleans L'Union, 1862

New Orleans Republican, 1867

New Orleans Times, 1863–66

Bibliography

New Orleans Tribune, 1864–66
New York Times, 1862, 1865–66, 1884, 1886
Liberator, 1865
Nation, 1866

ARTICLES AND PAMPHLETS

Abell, William Russell. "Judge Edmund Abell and the New Orleans Riots of 1866." Des Moines, Iowa, 1986, typescript in New Orleans Public Library.

The American Fire Alarm and Police Telegraph. New Orleans: Clark & Brisbin, 1859.

"The Architecture of James Gallier, Jr." *Gallier House* 4 (Fall 1983): 1–2.

Burns, Francis P. "White Supremacy in the South: The Battle for Constitutional Government in New Orleans, July 30, 1866." *Louisiana Historical Quarterly* 18 (July 1935): 581–616.

Connor, William P. "Reconstruction Rebels: The *New Orleans Tribune* in Post-War Louisiana." *Louisiana History* 21 (Spring 1980): 159–81.

Dawson, Joseph G. "General Phil Sheridan and Military Reconstruction in Louisiana." *Civil War History* 24 (June 1978): 133–51.

Dostie, A[nthony] P[aul]. *Address of Dr. A. P. Dostie delivered before the Republican Association of New Orleans, May 9, 1866.* New Orleans[?]: N.p., 1866[?].

Field, Beatrice M. "Potpourri: An Assortment of Tulane's People and Places." New Orleans: Tulane Library Special Collections typescript, August 1983.

Helis, Thomas W. "Of Generals and Jurists: The Judicial System of New Orleans Under Union Occupation, May 1862–April 1865." *Louisiana History* 29 (Spring 1988): 143–62.

Joshi, Manoj K., and Joseph P. Reidy. "To Come Forward and Aid in Putting Down This Unholy Rebellion": The Officers of Louisiana's Free Black Native Guard During the Civil War Era." *Southern Studies* 11 (1982): 326–42.

Logsdon, Joseph, and Caryn Cossé Bell. "The Americanization of Black New Orleans, 1850–1900." In *Creole New Orleans: Race and Americanization,* edited by Arnold R. Hirsch and Joseph Logsdon. Baton Rouge: Louisiana State University Press, 1992.

Lowrey, Walter M. "The Political Career of James Madison Wells." *Louisiana Historical Quarterly* 31 (October 1948): 995–1123.

McConnell, Roland C. "Louisiana's Black Military History." In *Louisiana's Black Heritage,* edited by Robert R. MacDonald, John R. Kemp, and Edward F. Haas. New Orleans: Louisiana State Museum, 1979.

Moore, W. G. "Notes of Colonel W. G. Moore, Private Secretary to President Johnson, 1866–1868." *American Historical Review* 19 (October 1913): 98–132.

The New Orleans Riot: "My Policy" in Louisiana. Washington, D.C.: Daily Morning Chronicle, 1866.

Nott, J. C. "Climates of the South in Their Relations to White Labor." *De Bow's Review* 1 (February 1866): 166–73.

Padgett, James A. "Some Letters of George Stanton Denison, 1854–1866: Observations of a Yankee on Conditions in Louisiana and Texas." *Louisiana Historical Quarterly* 23 (October 1940): 1132–1240.

Pierce, Charles W. *Jotham Warren Horton: In Memoriam.* Boston[?]: N.p., 1892[?].

Proceedings of the Convention of the Republican Party of Louisiana. New Orleans: Tribune Office, 1865.

Shewmaker, Kenneth E., and Andrew K. Prinz, eds. "A Yankee in Louisiana: Selections from the Diary and Correspondence of Henry R. Gardner, 1862–1866." *Louisiana History* 5 (Summer 1964): 271–95.

Simpson, Amos E., and Vaughn Baker. "Michael Hahn: Steady Patriot." *Louisiana History* 13 [Summer 1972]: 229–52.

Some Remarks upon the Proposed Election of February 22d. New Orleans[?]: N.p., 1864[?].

Somers, Dale A. "Black and White in New Orleans: A Study in Urban Race Relations, 1865–1900." *Journal of Southern History* 40 (February 1974): 19–42.

Summers, Mark W. "The Moderates' Last Chance: The Louisiana Election of 1865." *Louisiana History* 24 (Winter 1983): 49–70.

Tregle, Joseph G. "Thomas J. Durant, Utopian Socialism, and the Failure of Presidential Reconstruction in Louisiana." *Journal of Southern History* 45 (November 1979): 485–512.

Uzee, Philip D. "The Beginnings of the Louisiana Republican Party." *Louisiana History* 12 (Summer 1971): 197–211.

Vandal, Gilles. "The Origins of the New Orleans Riot of 1866, Revisited." *Louisiana History* 22 (Spring 1981): 135–65.

Books

Baird, John A., Jr. *Profile of a Hero: The Story of Absalom Baird, His Family, and the American Military Tradition.* Philadelphia: Dorrance, 1977.

Basler, Roy P., ed. *The Collected Works of Abraham Lincoln.* 9 vols. New Brunswick, N.J.: Rutgers University Press, 1953–55.

Beale, Howard K. *The Critical Year: A Study of Andrew Johnson and Reconstruction.* New York: Frederick Ungue, 1958.

Bell, Caryn Cossé. *Revolution, Romanticism, and the Afro-Creole Protest Tradition in Louisiana, 1718–1868.* Baton Rouge: Louisiana State University Press, 1997.

Belz, Herman. *Reconstructing the Union: Theory and Policy During the Civil War.* Ithaca, N.Y.: Cornell University Press, 1969.

Bergeron, Arthur W. *Guide to Louisiana Confederate Military Units, 1861–1865.* Baton Rouge: Louisiana State University Press, 1989.

Black, Earl, and Merle Black. *Politics and Society in the South.* Cambridge, Mass.: Harvard University Press, 1987.

Booth, Andrew B. *Records of Louisiana Confederate Soldiers and Louisiana Confederate Commands.* 3 vols. 1920; rpr., Spartanburg, S.C.: Reprint Co., 1984.

Bowers, Charles G. *The Tragic Era: The Revolution After Lincoln.* Boston: Houghton Mifflin, 1957.

Brock, W. R. *An American Crisis: Congress and Reconstruction, 1865–1867.* New York: Harper Torchbooks, 1963.

Butler, Benjamin Franklin. *Private and Official Correspondence of Gen. Benjamin F. Butler During a Period of the Civil War.* 5 vols. Edited by Jessie Ames Marshall. Norwood, Mass.: Plimpton Press, 1917.

Carter, Dan T. *When the War Was Over: The Failure of Self-Reconstruction in the South, 1865–1867.* Baton Rouge: Louisiana State University Press, 1985.

Chase, John Churchill. *Frenchmen, Desire, Good Children, and Other Streets of New Orleans,* 3d ed. New York: Simon & Schuster, 1997.

Chase, Salmon P. "Diary and Correspondence of Salmon P. Chase." *Annual Report of the American Historical Association; The Year 1902.* Washington, D.C.: U.S. Government Printing Office, 1903.

Conrad, Glenn R., ed. *A Dictionary of Louisiana Biography.* 2 vols. New Orleans: Louisiana Historical Association in cooperation with the Center for Louisiana Studies, 1988.

Cook, Adrian. *The Armies of the Streets: The New York City Draft Riots of 1863.* Lexington: University of Kentucky Press, 1974.

[Corsan, W. C.] *Two Months in the Confederate States, Including a Visit to New Orleans under the Dominion of General Butler.* London: Richard Bentley, N.p., 1863.

Cox, LaWanda. *Lincoln and Black Freedom: A Study in Presidential Leadership.* Columbia: University of South Carolina Press, 1981.

Cox, LaWanda, and John H. Cox. *Politics, Principle, and Prejudice, 1865–1866: Dilemma of Reconstruction America.* New York: Free Press of Glencoe, 1963.

Dawson, Joseph G. *Army Generals and Reconstruction: Louisiana, 1862–1877.* Baton Rouge: Louisiana State University Press, 1982.

Donald, David. *Charles Sumner and the Rights of Man.* New York: Knopf, 1970.

———. *The Politics of Reconstruction, 1863–1867.* Baton Rouge: Louisiana State University Press, 1965.

Du Bois, W. E. B. *Black Reconstruction in America.* New York: Russell & Russell, 1962.

Dutton, Geoffrey. *The Hero as Murderer: The Life of Edward John Eyre, Australian Explorer and Governor of Jamaica, 1815–1901.* London: William Collins, 1967.

Dyer, John P. *Tulane: The Biography of a University, 1834–1965.* New York: Harper & Row, 1966.

Foner, Eric. *Nothing but Freedom: Emancipation and Its Legacy.* Baton Rouge: Louisiana State University Press, 1983.

———. *Reconstruction: America's Unfinished Revolution, 1863–1877.* New York: Harper & Row, 1988.

Gardner's New Orleans Directory for 1866. New Orleans: Charles Gardner, 1866.

Bibliography

Gardner's *New Orleans Directory for 1867*. New Orleans: Charles Gardner, 1867.

Gillette, William. *Retreat from Reconstruction, 1869–1879*. Baton Rouge: Louisiana State University Press, 1979.

Grantham, Dewey W. *The Life and Death of the Solid South: A Political History*. Lexington: University Press of Kentucky, 1988.

Grimshaw, Allen D. *Racial Violence in the United States*. Chicago: Aldine, 1969.

Haller, John S. *Outcasts from Evolution: Scientific Attitudes of Racial Inferiority, 1859–1900*. Urbana: University of Illinois Press, 1971.

Harrington, Fred Harvey. *Fighting Politician: Major General N. P. Banks*. Philadelphia: University of Pennsylvania Press, 1948.

Hepworth, George H. *The Whip, Hoe, and Sword; or, The Gulf-Department in '63*. Boston: Walker, Wise, 1864.

Hollandsworth, James G. *The Louisiana Native Guards: The Black Military Experience in the Civil War*. Baton Rouge: Louisiana State University Press, 1995.

———. *Pretense of Glory: The Life of General Nathaniel P. Banks*. Baton Rouge: Louisiana State University Press, 1998.

Horsman, Reginald. *Josiah Nott of Mobile: Southerner, Physician, and Racial Theorist*. Baton Rouge: Louisiana State University Press, 1987.

Houzeau, Jean-Charles. *My Passage at the New Orleans* Tribune: *A Memoir of the Civil War Era*. Edited by David G. Rankin, translated by Gerard F. Denault. Baton Rouge: Louisiana State University Press, 1984.

Kendall, John Smith. *History of New Orleans*. Chicago: Lewis, 1922.

McCrary, Peyton. *Abraham Lincoln and Reconstruction: The Louisiana Experiment*. Princeton, N.J.: Princeton University Press, 1978.

McPherson, James M. *The Negro's Civil War: How American Blacks Felt and Acted During the War for the Union*. 1965; rpr. New York: Ballantine, 1991.

———. *The Struggle for Equality: Abolitionists and the Negro in the Civil War and Reconstruction*. Princeton, N.J.: Princeton University Press, 1964.

Nicolay, John G., and John Hay. *Abraham Lincoln: A History*. 10 vols. New York: Century, 1914.

Overdyke, W. Darrell. *The Know-Nothing Party in the South*. Baton Rouge: Louisiana State University Press, 1950.

Phillips, Ulrich Bonnell. *American Negro Slavery: A Survey of the Supply, Employment and Control of Negro Labor as Determined by the Plantation Regime*. 1918; rpr. Baton Rouge: Louisiana State University Press, 1966.

Pratt, Fletcher. *Stanton: Lincoln's Secretary of War*. New York: Norton, 1953.

Rable, George C., *But There Was No Peace: The Role of Violence in the Politics of Reconstruction*. Athens: University of Georgia Press, 1984.

Reed, Emily Hazen. *Life of A. P. Dostie; or, The Conflict in New Orleans*. New York: Wm. P. Tomlinson, 1868.

Reinders, Robert C. *End of an Era: New Orleans, 1850–1860*. New Orleans: Pelican, 1964.

Riddleberger, Patrick W. *1866: The Critical Year Revisited.* Carbondale: Southern Illinois University Press, 1979.

Ripley, C. Peter. *Slaves and Freedmen in Civil War Louisiana.* Baton Rouge: Louisiana State University Press, 1976.

Rose, Willie Lee. *Rehearsal for Reconstruction: The Port Royal Experiment.* Indianapolis: Bobbs-Merrill, 1964.

Rousey, Dennis C. *Policing the Southern City: New Orleans, 1805–1889.* Baton Rouge: Louisiana State University Press, 1996.

Sefton, James E. *Andrew Johnson and the Uses of Constitutional Power.* Boston: Little, Brown, 1980.

————. *The United States Army and Reconstruction, 1865–1877.* Baton Rouge: Louisiana State University Press, 1967.

Soulé, Leon Cyprian. *The Know Nothing Party in New Orleans: A Reappraisal.* Baton Rouge: Thomas J. Moran's Sons for the Louisiana Historical Association, 1961.

Taylor, Joe Gray. *Louisiana: A Bicentennial History.* New York: Norton in association with the American Association for State and Local History, 1976.

————. *Louisiana Reconstructed, 1863–1877.* Baton Rouge: Louisiana State University Press, 1974.

Thomas, Benjamin P., and Harold M. Hyman. *Stanton: The Life and Times of Lincoln's Secretary of War.* New York: Knopf, 1962.

Trefousse, Hans L. *Historical Dictionary of Reconstruction.* New York: Greenwood Press, 1991.

Trelease, Allen W. *White Terror: The Ku Klux Klan Conspiracy and Southern Reconstruction.* Baton Rouge: Louisiana State University Press, 1971.

Tunnell, Ted. *Crucible of Reconstruction: War, Radicalism and Race in Louisiana, 1862–1877.* Baton Rouge: Louisiana State University Press, 1984.

Vandal, Gilles. *Anatomy of a Tragedy: The New Orleans Riot of 1866.* Lafayette, La.: Center for Louisiana Studies, 1986.

Warner, Ezra J. *Generals in Blue: Lives of the Union Commanders.* Baton Rouge: Louisiana State University Press, 1964.

[Whitaker, Judge]. *Sketches of Life and Character in Louisiana.* New Orleans: Ferguson & Crosby, 1847.

White, Howard A. *The Freedmen's Bureau in Louisiana.* Baton Rouge: Louisiana State University Press, 1970.

Williams, T. Harry. *Huey Long.* New York: Knopf, 1969.

Wooster, Ralph A. *The Secession Conventions of the South.* Princeton, N.J.: Princeton University Press, 1962.

Index